THE OLD TOWN HALL (RATHAUS) OF NUREMBERG

FROM AN ENGRAVING, DATED 1614, IN THE NUREMBERG TOWN LIBRARY

First published in 1928 by D. Appleton and Company
First Skyhorse Publishing edition, 2015

Skyhorse Publishing books may be purchased in bulk at special discounts for sales promotion, corporate gifts, fund-raising, or educational purposes. Special editions can also be created to specifications. For details, contact the Special Sales Department, Skyhorse Publishing, 307 West 36th Street, 11th Floor, New York, NY 10018 or info@skyhorsepublishing.com.

Skyhorse® and Skyhorse Publishing® are registered trademarks of Skyhorse Publishing, Inc.®, a Delaware corporation.

Visit our website at www.skyhorsepublishing.com.

10 9 8 7

Library of Congress Cataloging-in-Publication Data is available on file.

Cover design by Jane Sheppard
Cover illustration "The Execution of Hans Fröschel by Master Franz Schmidt," State Archives of Nuremberg

Print ISBN: 978-1-62914-480-1
Ebook ISBN: 978-1-62914-976-9

Printed in China

CONTENTS

LIST OF ILLUSTRATIONS

vii.

A BRIEF ACCOUNT OF
CRIMINAL PROCEDURE IN GERMANY
IN THE MIDDLE AGES

by

C. CALVERT

A BRIEF ACCOUNT OF
CRIMINAL PROCEDURE IN GERMANY
IN THE MIDDLE AGES

I. THE JAIL

BETWEEN 1616–22 the Nuremberg Rathaus was, to a large extent, enlarged or rebuilt, and further important additions were made during the second half of the nineteenth century ; but the dungeons that honeycombed the foundations of the ancient structure have survived almost unaltered. A few cells retain some of their original fittings ; it is therefore possible to form an accurate idea of the way in which law-breakers were housed inside the *Loch*, when this was the principal jail of the City and Ban of Nuremberg.

Here, during those centuries, thousands of sinners and, unfortunately, not a few innocent people, spent weeks, months, or even years, in gloomy, underground cells, the horrors of which were aggravated by dampness, vermin, foul air, and defective sanitation. So bad were the conditions that prisoners released after any considerable term of confinement were found to be broken in health and often mentally enfeebled. Feuchtwanger's *Jew Süss* gives a detailed, and not overdrawn, description of the effect that similar treatment had on a vigorous man in the prime of life.

The harsh fashion in which law-givers punished crime was, however, regarded with apathy by the public, who apparently considered imprisonment, whether wrongly or rightly inflicted, as one of the chances of fortune, or one of the many crosses laid on mankind by Heaven ; a misfortune that might befall anyone, and which must, therefore, be borne patiently. Guests at the sumptuous banquets and entertainments given in the splendid Hall of the Rathaus were not troubled by compassion for the poor wretches lingering, often enough under sentence of death, in the dark cells only a few yards below.

Bad as was the Nuremberg jail, it long compared favourably with most contemporary prisons, either in Germany or elsewhere. Those of the neighbouring towns, Bornheim, Frankfurt, Mainz, and Landau, were assuredly no better ; but the Nuremberg Government appears to have lagged behind in this respect, for a report on the *Loch*, published in 1799, states that in no other prison of the time were conditions so wretched. Everything was out of date ; the cells still dark, damp, insanitary, infested with vermin ; cleaned, at most, twice a month ; and during the winter insufficiently warmed by braziers of burning charcoal, the fumes of which half suffocated the inmates. Medical attendance and spiritual consolation were almost entirely lacking, even for those who were in urgent need of them. Prisoners, many of them heavily ironed round the waist and at the feet, were confined for years, often together with their innocent children. Visitors and all means of passing away the time were still forbidden, as in the worst mediæval times. And yet, centuries before, the Karolina Code had expressly laid down that imprisonment should serve merely to secure the person, and not as a means of torture.

The *Loch* consists of a maze of passages,

lighted, if at all, by narrow, barred windows. In these passages are sixty wooden doors, iron-lined, some of them bearing numbers. On one is the picture of a crowing cock, coloured fiery red ; from which it is supposed that incendiaries were imprisoned there. On another door is painted a black cat, possibly because the cell was used to confine those under suspicion of magic or of witchcraft.

The masonry is of rough stone, and the cells measure, on the average, between nine and ten feet in length, about eight in breadth, and ten feet or so to the top of the vaulted roof. Originally the walls were bare, but later they were lined with heavy planks, which, as they did not follow the curve of the roof, considerably diminished the air space. Along the wall facing the entrance, at the height of approximately two feet from the floor, is a wooden shelf or bunk about a yard wide. A bench, also of wood, occupies one side of the apartment. In addition, the cells were formerly provided with a large, wooden, sanitary bucket, fitted with a lid that served as a table.

In the passage leading to the Torture Chamber

are three larger apartments, the condemned cells. To these, after receiving sentence of death, prisoners were transferred and watched day and night to prevent suicide or attempts to escape. In one of these cells, besides the usual shelf, bench, and bucket, is a table on which the felon's last meal was laid.

Another apartment contains the Stocks, an instrument freely employed, not only for the correction of ordinary rogues, but also to extract information from prisoners of war, unless such captives happened to be of good standing, and therefore valuable for the purposes of ransom or of exchange. The sanitary arrangements provided with this machine show that some of those who were locked in it suffered for days on end. It was customary to put such patients on short rations.

A narrow passage, formerly kept locked when not in use, leads to the surprisingly small and narrow Torture Chamber. In it we see a windlass and a wooden frame, furnished with a roller. Over this ran a rope to which the prisoner was fastened and then hoisted aloft with wooden, or stone, weights hanging to his feet. On the

wall is a board bearing the sinister words :
Male patratis sunt atra theatra parata. Formerly
there were two torture chambers ; but one was
suppressed to provide an extra room for the
Head Jailer.

The prison contained a repairing shop, by
means of which, among other things, the
torture instruments were kept in good order.
There was also a bathroom, but this was so
little used that its very existence seems to have
been forgotten for a time. The few who benefited by it were those suffering from wounds
received under torture, as well as prisoners who
had contracted skin diseases and other com-
plaints by reason of the damp and filth of the
cells. These were so unhealthy that several
entries record special grants of clothing to
captives whose garments had rotted on them
during confinement.

The only bed provided was the wooden shelf ;
no more than a rough blanket or a pelt was
allowed for covering, even in the coldest weather.
Charcoal braziers, serving also as fumigators,
warmed the jail during the winter. The cells
were not cleaned regularly ; at the beginning of

the seventeenth century a chronicle notes with astonishment that on the occasion of a general cleaning of the *Loch*, all the prisoners had been temporarily removed from their cells.

Oil lamps, hung in niches along the corridors, faintly lighted the gloom ; but sometimes, when a visit of the authorities was expected, wax tapers were provided, either in place of or in addition to the lamps.

The Head Jailer, *Lochhüter*, or *Lochwirt*, or, in felons' jargon, ' The Landlord of the Green Frog,' was a very responsible person. On appointment he was required to deposit caution money, and, occasionally, also to find respectable burghers as sureties. He, his family, and his servants were compelled to take an oath of fidelity. Head Jailers were expected to rule their charges severely, and had a free hand in any measures they chose to adopt ; therefore should the *Lochhüter* be of a brutal disposition, the prisoners' lot was hard. No odium attached to the post ; in 1474 the mother of a Head Jailer was granted the freedom of the City.

As early as the middle of the fifteenth century

Jailer's work was, therefore, heavy. Besides being responsible for the custody, the board, and the health of the inmates, it was his duty to see that, on arrival, prisoners were searched for hidden weapons, or instruments; to take charge of any valuables or money the newcomers brought with them, and to lay out for the benefit of those confined in the jail such sums as they or their friends contributed towards extra comforts. He was further expected to provide the Council with detailed reports on everything that took place inside the *Loch*; to notify and superintend necessary repairs; as well as to undertake the preliminary examination of prisoners accused of lighter misdemeanours. Occasionally, too, he acted as witness at a trial or enquiry. In early times it was he who supplied the *stärkenden Trunk*, or strengthening draught, to the condemned on their last journey. Later, this duty was, out of respect for the Head Jailer's office, transferred to the executioner's assistant.

In return for his services he received a good salary and free quarters, which, however, consisted of two rooms only, one above the other; a third was afterwards added.

Prisoners were roughly divided into three classes : (1) Very serious offences ; (2) Serious offences ; (3) Light offences.

In the first two classes, according to the degree of their criminality, were placed those accused of treason, murder, sexual crimes, highway robbery, incendiarism, etc. For all these the usual punishment was death, by methods that varied with the gravity of the offence.

Thieves (if their crime was a first offence, and the value of the stolen goods did not amount to one florin), roysterers, idle or unruly apprentices, destitute people, especially if they were aliens, formed the third class ; offenders who, on conviction, were punished by whipping, branding, maiming, fining, or banishment, either for a number of years, or even for life. At one period, as an aggravation of the sentence of banishment, some felons were sent for a certain time to the Hungarian frontier prisons, or to serve on board the Genoese galleys.

Unfortunately, those who had no visible means of subsistence, particularly if they were foreigners, often ranked as criminals of the first or second class, and were imprisoned in the more remote and more unhealthy cells. Usually, too, they were heavily ironed. There was a marked and deplorable tendency to treat the destitute and the alien more harshly than the wealthy and the native born.

Great efforts were made to prevent prisoners from communicating with one another; and the Head Jailer continually received instructions to use strict supervision and to punish offenders of this kind severely. All measures, however, proved unavailing. Communication was carried on, chiefly by means of code messages tapped out on doors or walls, and by notes thrown through the ventilator openings and the spy holes in the doors; nor did the use of gratings prevent the practice.

As a rule prisoners were not allowed any occupation or the means of passing the time, although we hear of one who possessed a book, and of another who taught himself to read and write while serving his term.

The jail fare, except in cases where a bread and water diet was inflicted as punishment, seems to have been reasonably good. Those who could afford them were allowed luxuries to a limited extent. Thus, in 1541 the Head Jailer received orders not to supply any of his charges with more than one measure of wine daily.

Whenever possible the prisoner was expected to bear the expenses of his confinement ; and if he could not pay at once, to sign an undertaking that he would do so as soon as possible. The Head Jailer assessed the amount due ; usually he charged high prices, so much so that prisoners were allowed to demand an enquiry into the justice of the claim, with the result that they sometimes obtained a reduction of the bill. Destitute prisoners were looked on with dis- favour ; their keep was defrayed by benevolent institutions, and by sums contributed from the Town coffers.

Sick prisoners were permitted to have medical treatment and some comforts. The nursing and the extra expense were undertaken by religious sisterhoods, who drew on charitable funds, to which the Town Council also added not ungenerously. Serious cases of illness were sometimes transferred to the Head Jailer's quarters or, if necessary, to the healthier Turm prison.

Pregnant women, unless accused of very heinous crimes, were released, and in general the treatment accorded to female offenders was milder than that to which males were subjected.

Should a prisoner wish to draw up his will, or if he offered to make revelations considered likely to prove important, the Rathaus clerk, in the presence of trustworthy witnesses, took down the directions, or the depositions, through the closed door of the cell. It appears that jail-birds occasionally availed themselves of this privilege merely as a means of breaking the monotony of confinement.

Suicide was not uncommon, in spite of the zealous precautions taken to prevent it. To this end every prisoner was, on arrival, searched for weapons. and should he be suspected of the intention of taking his life a watch was set on him day and night. If he effected his purpose, the corpse was proceeded against in court as though the deceased were still living. Attempts at suicide met with sharp punishment.

An unpleasant feature of criminal procedure in Nuremberg and other mediæval governments

was the secrecy attached to it. These oligar-
chies, like all despotic governments, lived in a
state of suspicion, and constantly feared re-
prisals ; they therefore had recourse to mystery
as a means of striking additional terror, in spite
of the resentment this method roused among
free citizens. All officials were sworn to silence
regarding prisoners and everything that occurred
within the jail, and, most stringently, respecting
the place and date of approaching executions,
in order to baffle possible attempts at a rescue.
No unauthorised person, whatever his standing
or pretext, was allowed access to the *Loch*.
The penalty for disobedience was severe ; in
one instance the fact that the Head Jailer's
maid had admitted her lover within the prison
brought on her three years' banishment. Notwithstanding these deterrents the regulations
were frequently evaded, to the great annoyance
of the Council, which continually passed new
ordinances in the hope of suppressing these
abuses.

In spite of every precaution, such as setting
a special watch on those suspected of meditating
the attempt, prisoners occasionally escaped.

In 1580 a thief under sentence of death, after breaking through a couple of doors, the wall of a passage, and a ceiling, got safely away and covered his tracks so effectually that he was never recaptured. In circumstances of this kind the Head Jailer was liable to severe penalties ; one officer was executed on suspicion of having helped a prisoner to break out of jail.

The following regulations show the insecurity of those in power and the unsettled conditions of public safety in mediæval Nuremberg and the adjoining territories.

At every execution the spectators were warned that those who should endeavour to avenge the criminal would be liable to the same punishment as that inflicted on the condemned.

On release, prisoners were compelled to swear that they would not try to revenge themselves on the Council, or on its officers, for the treatment undergone. Often even this precaution was held to be insufficient ; and after he had taken the oath mentioned above the prisoner was banished for ever from the territory of Nuremberg. If he returned he was prosecuted on a charge of perjury, for which the punishment was death, mercilessly exacted from those who returned without leave, if they gave any grounds for complaint. In spite of this, so wretched was the condition of all but wealthy or influential aliens in most states during the Middle Ages, that many exiled men defied the gallows and returned to Nuremberg. Suspects against whom nothing could be proved were subjected to vexatious treatment. They had to undertake to remain in the City for a certain time, so that it would be easy to lay hands on them; or they might be required to find caution money, or sureties, or both, before they were even nominally released.

TORTURE was not a regular part of criminal procedure in early times, but it was firmly established as such by the beginning of the fourteenth century, and before the end of that period considerable sums were allotted for the purpose.

The introduction of this judicial method was gradual. In 1320 the *Leumund Privileg* empowered the Nuremberg Council to use torture as a means of extracting confessions, although the right of inflicting the death penalty still lay with the *Schultheiss*, or Imperial Judge, without whose consent all criminal proceedings were, theoretically, impossible. The *Privileg* of 1371 granted these powers to the Nuremberg *Rat*, so that the *Schultheiss* became in practice merely the servant of the City Council.

Private individuals were allowed to prosecute, but they could not take any part in the proceedings, beyond that of acting as witnesses;

they were also frequently called upon to bear the expenses of the trial.

Although prisoners charged with slight offences were often examined within the jail by the *Lochhüter*, in the majority of instances such an enquiry was conducted by the two *Lochschöffen* (prison magistrates), with the assistance of the prison clerk, who took down the minutes of the proceedings. As a rule this was held in a special room inside the Rathaus, but violent or otherwise dangerous felons were examined by the *Lochschöffen* in the jail itself.

By the beginning of the fifteenth century it was an established rule that all examinations of prisoners should be conducted exclusively by means of a series of questions which the Council itself had drawn up. These were at first few and simple, but ultimately developed into a set of questions numbering about a hundred. They dealt with the parentage, birthplace, nationality, standing and previous careers of the accused. Many questions were artfully framed so as to extract not only details as to the crime with which the prisoner was actually charged but also particulars regarding accomplices and former misdeeds. Should the examinee confess to any of the latter, even though he disavowed the offence for which he was being tried, his condemnation and punishment almost invariably followed. Only in rare instances were the *Lochschöffen* allowed to depart from the official list of questions; a practice that often hampered the examiners.

The *Lochschöffen* possessed no judicial authority; their duties were confined to the examination of prisoners and to drawing up a report on the proceedings. These reports were laid before the *Rat* at its next meeting, and that body decided on the steps to be taken. If the prisoner had confessed, he was condemned and the sentence carried out without delay. If he denied his guilt, he was subjected to a further examination, on which, should he still prove obstinate, torture was used to extract a confession.

Respectable burghers, women, and foreigners of good standing were seldom tortured. In the case of aliens, great consideration was given to the manner in which subjects of Nuremberg were treated in the states to which these foreigners belonged. Little mercy was shown to Jews and common criminals. The proceedings were as a rule carried out in secret, but when the victim was an alien, representatives of his nationality were sometimes allowed to be present.

The practice of torture, which had at first been an unusual expedient, became more and more frequent ; and by the end of the fifteenth century it seems to have been applied freely and ferociously, even on mere suspicion of complicity in a crime, till at last we find that it was considered immaterial whether the prisoner had been caught in the act or whether the accuser had withdrawn the charge. Torture was applied on the grounds that a person who had given cause for suspicion was likely to be one who would commit the crime laid against him, and that therefore it was expedient to make certain whether he was innocent even of complicity, and to discover possible partners in his crime. Immense importance was attached to confession of guilt or of complicity. Without such an avowal, in theory, no condemnation was possible ; and this partly explains the savage spirit in which torture was employed.

This principle was based on conscientious grounds, and harsh as were the Nuremberg law-makers, they adhered to it steadily, almost without exception. In 1452 when some neighbouring princes complained of its favouring the accused, in so far that such individuals could avoid penalties by refusing to confess, the Council replied they would rather ten guilty people escaped punishment by this means, than that one innocent person should suffer through being condemned without confession.

Nevertheless, in practice the method led to many miscarriages of justice ; for confession, however obtained, was deemed sufficient to warrant condemnation. Not only was it judged to be immaterial whether the evidence supported the confession, but the fact that it actually contradicted the avowal was also held to be equally unimportant. No weight was attached to the consideration that many poor wretches, unable to face the torture, confessed, declaring openly that they preferred death to such agony. Thus, in 1610 a woman accused of infanticide admitted the crime and named the place where she had buried the victim. Despite the fact that no remains were found at the spot indicated, she was executed ; the judges were most unwilling to condemn, but, as the law stood, her confession left them no alternative.

It is true that torture was not applied till prisoners had resisted all persuasion ; yet this was of no benefit to them ; for unless they owned to their guilt, tortured they were ; and though in a few instances the heroism of the accused defied every effort of his tormentors, only too often the innocent preferred death to the long protracted horrors of the torture chamber.

In early times the degree and method of torture was left to the judgment of the executioner and his assistant (*der Löwe*), who alone were allowed to inflict it ; but gradually both degree and method were reduced to a strict system.

The hangman and his subordinate were, as a rule, excluded from the torture chamber while the prisoner made his confession.

In no instance was torture applied till the

prisoner had refused to acknowledge his guilt at the first examination. Such criminals were transferred to the torture chamber, where the mere sight of the instruments often produced the desired avowal. If this was not sufficient, the accused was fastened to some instrument, and the executioner made a pretence of applying the torture. Should the patient still continue obdurate, punishment was inflicted in earnest.

As early as the fifteenth century the following methods were in regular use :

(1) The Thumb-screw and the Boot.
(2) The *Aufziehen*. In this torture the prisoner's hands were tied behind his back. Next, the executioner or his assistant fastened the sufferer's wrists to a rope that ran over a roller high overhead. By this means the sufferer was hoisted aloft. If it was considered necessary to increase the torture, wooden or stone weights of various sizes were attached to the victim's feet.
(3) The Ladder, on which prisoners were bound and stretched.

(4) Fire (*Feuer*); that is, lighted candles or torches, applied to the armpits.

(5) The *Fass*, a kind of cradle fitted with spikes, in which the patient was laid and rocked.

To these, in 1530, was added the *Kranz* or *Schneiden*, a strap or straps fastened round the head and gradually drawn close. In addition, the cat, branding, tweaking with red hot tongs, etc., were freely used, either as additions to capital punishment or for lighter offences. All these methods, or a combination of them, could be applied.

In a tower, one of the few surviving portions of the old City Castle, is a large collection of torture instruments. Many of these are foreign devices, and were never used in Nuremberg. The same may almost certainly be said of the famous ' Iron Maiden,' a hollow figure resembling a huge mummy coffin that towers among the ghastly contents of the room. The front portion of this machine consists of two parts working on hinges, and the interior is fitted with several

Legend has it that criminals were executed by being forced into the case, after which the hinged portions were gradually closed, thus transfixing the victim on the spikes.

Apart from a solitary and doubtful passage in the Chronicle of 1533, there is no evidence whatever to support this sensational tradition, which must certainly be false as regards some details ; for it declares that the enclosed corpse was ultimately cut to pieces by sharp blades mechanically driven, and that the fragments of flesh fell through the bottom of the case into a shaft, and so reached running water, where they became food for fishes. A casual glance at the machine will show that this statement is an impossibility ; nor are there any grounds for the belief that the instrument was employed as a means of terrorising criminals. For one thing, the chamber of the Rathaus in which alone torture was inflicted is too small to accommodate the bulky ' Maiden.'[1]

Prisoners were often tortured in batches, more especially if they belonged to a gang, in the hope that some of them would inform against

[1] See Mummenhoff's exhaustive enquiry on this point.

Das Frauen-Thor zu Nürnberg.

THE FRAUENTOR

FROM AN ENGRAVING BY GEORG CHRISTIAN EMMART, SECOND HALF OF 17TH CENTURY

TOWN LIBRARY AT NUREMBERG

(face p. 24)

their fellows. Torture could be repeated indefinitely even on mere suspicion, nor was the victim always allowed to recover from the effects of a previous application. Refusal to confess seemingly roused the authorities to positive savagery. A revolting instance of this occurred in 1599. The prisoner, after undergoing several applications, still refused to admit that he had been guilty of a certain crime, though he confessed to other misdeeds, all punishable with death, and on account of which he asked to be executed without further torture. Notwithstanding this, his mangled body was again tormented, twice with fire and four times with the rack in conjunction with the *kranz*. Even then the examiners could not wring from him the desired avowal; whereupon, though he piteously begged to be beheaded, he was broken on the wheel. This is not an isolated instance ; and during the next century the severity of the authorities so increased that the *feuer* and the *kranz* were often employed in dealing with ordinary thieves.

Many prisoners showed amazing courage under torture, and by refusing to confess occasionally baffled their persecutors ; though in the majority of such instances some pretext was discovered for executing the accused or for keeping him jailed in conditions so harsh that he died. One desperate felon vainly tried to shorten his sufferings by holding in his breath till death should result ; another, a thief, was seemingly so attached to Nuremberg, his native city, that he entreated the *Rat* to execute him rather than banish him ; as, having been a criminal from a child, he could not give up his evil practices nor live away from his native city.　The garotte settled his difficulties.

It is strange to find classed among the criminal cases such comparatively harmless sexual aberrations as that to which a young prisoner confessed :　namely that he had cut off the tresses of about one hundred girls.

The famous Muffel trial of 1469 was remarkable for the fact that this man, who had been accused of embezzling public money, was, though a citizen of standing, severely tortured. He claimed as a burgher to be exiled from the city, but the incensed Council condemned him to be garotted.

Oddly enough, the suspicious and severe *Rat* was comparatively lenient towards witches, unless these were convicted of gross swindling or of selling magic potions.

This harsh treatment of criminals and suspects was, in a measure, due to the general insecurity and to the small size of many Mid-European states, which facilitated the escape of law-breakers. Authorities were anxious to obtain information regarding prisoners, especially if these were aliens about whose antecedents, consequently, less was known. To this end a brisk correspondence was carried on between governments, in accordance with certain fixed principles, which represented a rudimentary form of international criminal law. When undertaking the prosecution of foreigners, the authorities could generally rely on the assistance of the state to which such people belonged ; and the state in question was frequently requested to undertake the trial and to defray the expenses connected with these prosecutions.

As public safety improved and more humane ideas spread, the use of torture diminished, and by the end of the sixteenth century it was a recognised, though not universally observed, principle that judgment might be passed independently of confession on the part of the accused. The evidence of three trustworthy eyewitnesses was held to be sufficient, thus doing away with the necessity of employing torture. Mere suspicion, also, was no longer deemed to be adequate grounds for passing the death sentence, though it was still considered to justify the use of torture in order to extract a confession. Moreover, as early as 1521 it was decreed that if those who had confessed under torture subsequently retracted the confession, they were not to be tortured afresh, unless further proofs of guilt were forthcoming; but these merciful provisions were, in practice, frequently overridden.

Strangely enough, although unjust imprisonment was, in a few instances, considered worthy of money compensation, no such indemnity seems ever to have been granted for sufferings undergone in the torture chamber.

III. THE EXAMINATION AND TRIAL

DURING the early Middle Ages, trials were held publicly in the market place, and anyone who chose could follow the proceedings. These were directed by the Emperor's legal representative, the *Schultheiss*, assisted by the *Schöffen*.

As a preliminary, an official, the *Richter*, enquired whether all formalities necessary to constitute a lawful tribunal had been observed ; thus, among other details, whether the trial was being held on the day and between the hours appointed for legal proceedings, and whether the *Schöffen's* bench was occupied by the proper officials. After this a beadle or usher summoned the accuser and defendant to appear.

From the city records it seems that during the twelfth and thirteenth centuries it was considered essential to successful prosecutions that criminals should have been caught in the act, or immediately after.

The prosecutor's task was unpleasant and

dangerous ; especially when the offence was murder or theft ; for on witnessing the crime he was expected to raise the cry of " mörderio ! " (murder) or " dibio ! " (thief), and with the help of bystanders to seize the offender. The next step was to secure evidence of the outrage, such as the hand or finger of the murdered person, or, in dealing with a theft, some at least of the stolen goods. These objects were fastened to the culprit's back, and to the shout of " mörderio ! " or " dibio ! " he was dragged before the authorities. If the prisoner denied the charge, recourse was had to the *Übersiebnen*[1], that is the accuser took an oath that the crime had been committed or attempted, and supported his statement by producing six *Eidhelfer*, that is six respectable citizens, who, under oath, declared that in their opinion the accusation was true and made without malice on the part of the accuser. Condemnation followed, and the sentence was at once carried out.

If the culprit could not be arrested in the act, the prosecutor, with the least possible delay, laid the evidence of the crime before the court,

[1] Similar to the Anglo-Saxon method of compurgation.

demanding a trial ; and the accused, when captured, was dealt with as if he had been caught red-handed. Should the accused surrender voluntarily, the matter might, in certain circumstances, be decided by ordeal, or by duel.

Any delay in the prosecution favoured the accused, so much so that he was granted a safe conduct to the court, and often allowed to clear himself by merely taking an oath of innocence.

In early times accusations unsupported by material evidence, and based on bare suspicion or on evil report, were not considered justifiable grounds for legal action. An important alteration was made in 1281, when the *Rudolfinischer Landfriede* laid down the principle that a suspect might be prosecuted and condemned, provided six " good men and true " declared under oath that in their opinion he was a dangerous person.

By 1294, although the prosecutor was still expected to bring the accused bound into court, it was of no moment whether the felon had or had not been caught in the act, or whether some time had elapsed before the accusation was brought ; nor was it necessary to produce material evidence. The prosecutor must, however, be a reputable person and give surety that he intended to carry the prosecution through ; whereupon a day was appointed for the trial. At this the accuser was provided with a counsel, who does not seem to have been necessarily a skilled lawyer, since he was allowed to claim that any mistake made by him through ignorance of the code must not be prejudicial to the prosecutor. If the accused denied the charge, the prosecution produced, as in former times, six supporters (*Eidhelfer*). These were not required to have witnessed the crime, but merely to swear that in their judgment the charge was just and not maliciously brought. The only defence possible for the accused was to challenge the respectability of the six *Eidhelfer*. If he could not do so successfully, the *Schöffen* declared in favour of the prosecutor, at the same time warning the public that any attempt at revenge on the part of the accused's supporters would be punished as severely as the crime itself. The sentence followed, and was carried out with all possible despatch.

Nevertheless, if the accused were a citizen, and

took an oath that he was innocent, we find that unless the crime were very serious, proceedings were dropped. In certain circumstances, as a compromise, the accused was compelled to leave the state, and warned that if he came back without permission the trial would not be re-opened, but that he would be treated as a felon guilty of the offence for which he had been banished.

Should the prosecutor have killed the accused in the attempt to capture him, the former was compelled to swear that it had not been possible to secure the latter otherwise, and the court proceeded against the deceased as if he had been alive.

Till 1320, the power of condemning to death lay with the *Schultheiss* alone, but in that year the *Leumund Privileg* invested the Town Council with this right, which in 1323 was further enlarged by the proviso that, should the Imperial Representative refuse to act, the Council might do so independently. In these circumstances, oddly enough, the *Löwe* (or hangman's assistant) acted as the public accuser. During the next century a very marked change was introduced.

Confession became all important, whether voluntary or extracted by torture. The City records certainly prove that the authorities showed a praiseworthy conscientiousness in endeavouring to secure evidence to supplement confession; but evidence was not considered necessary. Confession remained as the one condition on which a man should be condemned, and to secure it all means were held to be justifiable. Consequently the employment of *Übersiebnen* became superfluous and grew obsolete.

The confession, together with any corroborating evidence, was submitted to *Konsulenten*, advisory jurists trained in the Italian schools of law. They weighed the matter and reported their opinion to the Council, who as a rule passed judgment accordingly.

By this time trials no longer took place in the market square, but in a special hall within the Rathaus, after the accused had been privately examined. The change was much resented by the burghers, who for many a year, as the famous Muffel case shows, rebelled against the secrecy of the new method. By 1478 the following procedure was in force:

The criminal, bound and wearing the felon's garb (white, blue, or black), appeared in court. If he confessed, he was at once condemned ; if he denied the charge, the *Lochschöffen* declared under oath that the man had confessed in their presence at the private examination, and unless the accused could disprove this statement, judgment followed. Should the criminal have died before the trial, the fettered corpse was produced in court. The *Richter*, or president, called on the dead man to appoint an advocate. As the accused was unable to do so the prosecutor proceeded to surmise that the man was dead, whereupon two *Schöffen* viewed the body and verified the decease. When they had done so the corpse was provided with an advocate, who, on the grounds that his client was not in full possession of his faculties, demanded the assistance of a *Schöffe*, with whom he discussed the charge and tried to defend his client's innocence. After he had finished, the court passed judgment. This gruesome farce was abandoned in 1526, when the law pronounced that it was unseemly to prosecute the dead.

Later, under the Karolina Code, the proceedings were as follows :

Having examined the documents and evidence, the *Konsulenten* submitted their opinion to the Council, which almost invariably accepted their findings. The *Bannrichter* with two *Schöffen* then went down to the jail, ordered the prisoner to be brought before them unbound, read the confession to him, and informed him that the trial would take place in three days. The accused was thereupon transferred to the condemned cell and warned to consider his soul's welfare. The prison chaplain visited him, and the warders assisted in exhorting him to repentance. He was allowed a liberal table, provided by charitable people, and visitors had free access to him.

On the morning of the Trial (or Judgment day) the Council met in the *Ratstube* to confirm or modify the sentence. This settled, the *Schöffen*, wearing their official robes, went to the Great Hall, where the *Bannrichter* was installed on a raised seat behind gratings of brass. Orders were given to produce the prisoner in court. The executioner knocked at the door of the condemned cell, entered, apologising for the intrusion, bound the prisoner's arms, cast a white cloak about the victim, and led him between two chaplains to the Judgment Hall. Here the *Bannrichter* enquired of the *Schöffen* whether the judgment passed were in conformity with the law. Having received assurance of this, he ordered the court clerk to read out the sentence, after which the condemned man was at once led out to execution.

IV. THE EXECUTIONER AND HIS ASSISTANT

DURING the earliest recorded years of the City's history the death penalty seems, after conviction, to have been carried out by the accuser, who strung up the criminal on any suitable tree or post. Sometimes, with an eye to poetic justice, the wrong-doer was made to suffer on the very spot where he had committed the crime. Such a method, however, was soon considered to be incompatible with the dignity of the court that had pronounced judgment; it also brought undesirable odium on the accuser; so that gradually the task devolved on the *Züchtiger*, an official entrusted with the infliction of torture and of other forms of punishment. The prosecutor was, nevertheless, required to provide or pay for the rope, the fuel for the pyre, and similar necessary items; a regulation that soon became obsolete in practice, although it figures on the statutes as late as the sixteenth century.

The executioner, known as the 'Mate of Death,' the *Hoher*, the *Haher*, the *Suspensor* and, later, as the *Henker*, *Nachrichter*, or, more commonly, the *Scharfrichter*, was a person of considerable importance as well as infamy. The City records show that it was difficult to find a skilled and, at the same time, reputable practitioner to fill the post. Many of those recruited were mere ruffians who themselves perished on the scaffold. Thus in 1386 Meister Friedrich was burnt alive at Windsheim as a coiner ; in 1479 Meister Hans was beheaded for treason by his assistant ; in 1503 an executioner killed his *Löwe* in the course of a quarrel over the rightful division of moneys received for despatching five criminals. On the other hand, in 1497 Meister Jorg, after many years of office, was made a freeman of the City. Some hangmen seem to have shown comparative humanity, for in 1507 Hans Peck earned a sharp reproof on account of the leniency with which he had treated a poor fellow condemned to the pillory. In 1525 Meister Gilg, having been commissioned to drown a woman convicted of infanticide,

he was allowed to do, on condition that both
left the City for good.

The office was not without its dangers. In
1544 hangman Kester was murdered in the
presence of a number of peasants, who made no
attempt to interfere with, still less to secure, the
murderer. It is therefore not surprising to
find that some artists, either on this account or
from the more respectable motive of humanity,
gave up their post.

From about 1350 we have a fairly complete
list of the Nuremberg executioners, together
with many details respecting their office and
careers. Perhaps the most famous, as well as
the most respectable of all the sinister list,
was Meister Franz Schmidt, author of the diary
from which are taken the entries translated
in this book. After acting for five years as
assistant to his father, who was executioner to
the Bishop of Bamberg, Schmidt settled in
Nuremberg, where he acted as chief *Scharfrichter*
from 1578 to 1617. During this period, according to his journal, he executed 361 persons and
otherwise punished 345 minor criminals; but
the record is incomplete.

Schmidt had some education, and also scientific tastes, which led him to dissect a number of his victims. He seems to have been superior to most who practised his revolting trade ; a stern man, but not altogether inhuman, and inspired by a grim piety, as his diary and Herr Keller's illuminating essay show. His disapproval of harsh punishment for those charged with witchcraft is to his credit, since every infliction of torture and each execution brought him heavy fees. Humane feelings also made him oppose the drowning of women, a practice that often entailed very protracted suffering. At his suggestion this method was changed into hanging or beheading, a swifter if equally stern procedure.

In 1585 he had the unpleasant duty of executing his brother-in-law by breaking him on the wheel. On his way to the gallows the criminal was punished with the red hot tongs. Only two tweaks were inflicted, the rest being remitted by the Council as a special favour, possibly out of regard for the presumed feelings of Schmidt. The two held a long and apparently edifying discourse on the Rabenstein, after which the condemned man was allowed to embrace his daughter. In the end the conscientious Franz despatched his relative with no less than thirty-one strokes of the bar. No entry relating to this execution is to be found in the diary, though some think that No. 88 may be a veiled record of the fact. In the circumstances the omission is not surprising.

In June 1603 Hans Spiss, either an intimate acquaintance of, or godfather to, Schmidt or to his children, was whipped out of the town because he was suspected of having connived at a murderer's escape. Schmidt enters the fact in his diary, adding significantly that his *Löwe* had administered the punishment. (*Diary, Part II, No.* 249.)

As a reward for his services, in 1584 Schmidt was granted full pay during life, and his lodgings were thoroughly renovated. He resigned in 1617, on which occasion he notes in his diary that he is once more a ' respectable ' person.

It would be interesting to know what were his feelings during the Thirty Years' War, for he lived on through half that stormy and lawless period. Probably he was consoled by the

thought that many ruffians who would otherwise have mounted the gallows were either
killed in battle or met their deserts at the hands
of a Provost Marshal. He died in 1634 and
was granted an honourable burial.

Another famous artist was Johann Michel
Widman, who practised for an almost incredible
period, 1665–1736, retaining his skill and vigour
to an advanced age ; for in 1717 he cut off the
head of a condemned man at a single stroke,
and at the same time almost severed the hands
of the *Löwe* who was holding the patient.

In the list of these officials we find the
Deublers, who are said to be connected with
the Deibler family, the famous Paris executioners. In the Nuremberg records it is stated
that Albanus Friedrich Deubler was practising
as hangman in that city during the first quarter
of the nineteenth century.

The office itself was considered disgraceful,
and although on one occasion an executioner's
mother, and in another instance an executioner
himself, received the freedom of the City, the
Scharfrichter, his assistants, and all people connected with him, were in bad repute ; so much

so that only as a special favour were they admitted to the sacraments.

As a trade the business was fairly profitable. The pay depended to a certain extent on the number of executions and of the tortures inflicted. The latter were paid at half the rate allowed for carrying out a capital sentence. In addition the hangman was usually granted a fixed salary and free lodgings in a house built on the stone arch of a bridge near the Henker-steg.[1] It was also customary to give him presents of money, especially at the New Year. Should a prisoner be respited, the executioner and his assistant received compensation.

Apart from this the *Scharfrichter* generally supplied some of the articles necessary to carry out his duties ; such as ropes, brimstone, wood, etc., and on these he was allowed to make a reasonable profit. Then, too, many of the craft practised surgery, and sold at a high price severed hands, human skin, and other ghastly relics valued by the superstitious for the purposes of magic, medicine, or the discovery of hidden treasure. One *Scharfrichter* earned

[1] See illustration facing page 75.

considerable sums as a letter-writer for the illiterate.

Satisfactory craftsmen were so hard to come by that a skilled and respectable artist could wring excellent terms from his employers, and continually did so in all manner of ways. For instance, in 1513 the executioner claimed and was granted as a perquisite the wooden platform used to drown criminals in the Pegnitz river.

As executions were carried out in public, it was important that they should not be bungled ; but mistakes were not infrequent, and on such occasions the *Scharfrichter* and his subordinate were often in danger at the hands of the crowd.

The *Löwe*, or hangman's assistant, was a remarkable personage. Originally he acted as a market policeman, who cleared the town of refuse, dead animals, diseased cattle, and adulterated goods. Making his rounds to the beat of a drum, he broke up groups of gamblers and roughs, buried unclaimed corpses, burnt the bodies of suicides, drummed the blasphemer out of the City, pilloried and branded criminals, and lent a hand to his chief in the Torture Chamber. Later, extraordinary as it may appear, he acted as public prosecutor, and even as magistrate (in cases where the *Schultheiss* refused to act), an office in which the *Löwe* was firmly established about 1487.

The term *Löwe* is, perhaps fantastically, supposed to be derived from the fact that in early times, as he helped to drag the prisoner before the judge, he uttered loud and threatening cries, and also because of the cruel fashion in which he handled the victims of torture. It is variously spelt *Löwe, Lewe, Lobe, Leve, Lew* ; occasionally, also, he is described as the *Peinlein* or *Freiknecht*.

The first official mention of him occurs in 1296, when he figures as the public prosecutor. Fuller powers were granted him by the *Privileg Kaiser Ludwig's* in 1323, by which the Town Council obtained from the Emperor independent authority to condemn. At one time the plan of appointing two such officials was discussed, but not sanctioned.

In 1494 an important change took place by which the *Löwe*, in the person of Jorg Gareis, was released from all duties connected with the policing of markets.

The *Löwe's* tenure of office seems to have been

more uncertain than that of the chief, like whom he was allowed a fixed salary. In addition he received for each execution or application of torture fees equal to half the amount granted to his superior for the same services. Substantial bonuses bestowed at the New Year and on other occasions further increased his salary.

The office was reputed dishonourable; a special decree was required in 1518 before the Thimble Makers would admit a *Löwe's* son to apprenticeship in their guild; and as in the case of the executioner, the sacrament was a favour rarely granted to the assistant. In 1580 law-court officials objected to standing near the *Löwe* at trials, and were allowed henceforward to keep apart from him.

When assisting his chief the *Löwe* carried out the more menial duties. It was he who fixed on the head of condemned Jews the cap smeared inside with pitch; who carried the pall, the keys of the gallows' enclosure, and the so-called 'strengthening draught' administered to criminals during their last moments. It was also the *Löwe* who, when the condemned suffered death by drowning, handled the pole with which the sack containing the victim was pressed and held below the surface.

Authorities who were temporarily or permanently without an executioner often borrowed the services of the *Scharfrichter* and the *Löwe* employed by a friendly adjoining state. The Nuremberg Council, like their neighbours, freely lent such officials, on condition that these men should be allowed to return without delay if their services were required at home. Excursions of this kind were handsomely rewarded, and proved a considerable source of revenue to the hangman and his assistant.

V. EXECUTIONS

AFTER the earliest period of the history of Nuremberg, the Köpfleinsberg, inside the City, seems to have been, with few exceptions, the place selected for the purpose of carrying out a death sentence. Later still, however, criminals usually suffered at one of two places outside the walls, that is, on the Rabenstein (ravens' stone) and on the Hochgericht (gallows).

The first was situated some two hundred yards south-east of the Frauentor, not far from the present Central Railway Station: the second lay about a quarter of a mile farther out in the same direction, near the district still known as the Galgenhof.

Both gallows consisted of massive stone platforms, on which rose the gibbet. The ' tree ' on the Hochgericht (or Hohes Gericht), built in 1441, was composed of several wooden uprights fitted with crossbeams, one of which projected considerably and was used to hang

Jews. Near this ponderous framework were two wheels employed to inflict the frightful punishment of Breaking on the Wheel. The following illustration, enlarged from a portion

of the photograph reproduced opposite, gives an interesting representation of this gibbet, from the projecting beam of which a Jew is seen suspended. Nearer in the foreground is the Unter Galgenhof.

The Rabenstein was the older of the two gallows, and by Schmidt's time had fallen into disuse. Though executions occasionally took

SECTION OF A PLAN OF NUREMBERG ABOUT 1590
SHOWING THE RABENSTEIN AND HOCHGERICHT

FROM A DRAWING BY PAUL PFINZING VON HENFENFELD
IN STATE ARCHIVES OF NUREMBERG

(face p. 50)

place there as late as in 1754, no trace of the structure is found in the eighteenth-century maps of Nuremberg.

Contemporary writers, perhaps with some touch of exaggeration, describe the gallows tree as in constant bearing; from it swung numerous corpses suspended in chains that rattled in the wind to a burden of croaking from the many ravens by which the place was haunted.

The woodwork, exposed to the raw winters of central Europe, needed constant attention and occasional rebuilding, such as was carried out in 1605. For this purpose 42 oak trunks were required; 25 master workmen, with the assistance of 335 ordinary hands and apprentices, were engaged on it. The largeness of the number of men employed is explained by the fact that, lest any odium should attach to those who executed the work, all suitable craftsmen within the Ban of Nuremberg were compelled to assist, and received full current wages for their labour. It appears that these men were exposed to horseplay from the crowd of onlookers, who went so far as to lasso some of the workmen. The matter was settled by a great drinking bout, in which the craftsmen and their persecutors shared, the expense being met by the former.

In 1749 the whole structure was once more completely decayed; it was rebuilt in six days and 'consecrated' with great ceremony. Occasionally executions were carried out in secret, some within the Rathaus or its precincts. In 1672 a Council treasurer was beheaded in a small yard near the Fünferhaus, probably because the Council did not wish the public to witness the disgrace of one of its officials. On this occasion a dummy scaffold was erected elsewhere, to deceive would-be spectators.

During the great wars of the sixteenth century at least one soldier belonging to the Imperial armies was beheaded on the Spitalkirchhof; others were hanged on a gibbet in the Pig Market, and during their occupation of Nuremberg the Swedes set up a military gallows for the punishment of their ruffianly troops. In ordinary times, however, soldiers suffered on one of the usual execution grounds; later, respect for the uniform made some distinction appear seemly; and after 1691 no military offender mounted the thieves' gallows.

At first it was customary for the hangman to accompany his victim from the prison to the place of execution, but subsequently this practice was discontinued; and as a rule the *Scharfrichter* left condemned men at the Kreuzgänglein and met them at the door of the gibbet platform.

On his last journey the felon, preceded by two mounted constables, walked or rode in a cart between two prison chaplains. Behind came the *Löwe* bearing the pall and the strong draught by which the patient was heartened and probably drugged. A *Richter* (magistrate) was also of the party; or else, in company with the executioner, received the doomed man at the entrance in the gallows' platform.

On the way a halt was made outside the City gate, and here the prisoner, if he was in a suitable frame of mind, received the sacrament. As a rule he wore the cloak of the condemned. Some went to death in their best clothing, as did the felon who put on a silk doublet for his last appearance. On one occasion a thief who had stolen linen was dressed for the scaffold in a costume of that material specially provided by the Bleachers' Guild.

The sick and the feeble were conveyed to execution in chairs ; heinous or violent criminals were drawn thither on an oxhide or on a wooden sledge (hurdle). In such cases it was considered a pious act to support the victim's head so as to prevent it from being bruised by the violent jolts. Members of charitable associations undertook this office. It would also appear that for conveying the condemned, carts were at times employed, drawn by horses borrowed from the night-soil workers' teams, to the indignation of these men. Apparently the animals were at one time ridden in a ribald fashion by several people, but later this practice was considered unseemly and strictly forbidden.

When the procession reached the door of the gallows' platform proclamation was made that anyone who should attempt to hinder or to avenge the execution would be most severely punished. The door was then unlocked, and the prisoner, together with some of the officials, mounted the steps to the gibbet and stood in full view of the crowd, before whom the executioner proceeded, with calculated deliberation, to complete his arrangements. In the meantime the victim made his peace with heaven, and occasionally addressed the public.

No block was used for beheading; the patient either stood, or sat, or knelt supported by the *Löwe*, who in consequence ran some risk if his principal made a slip.[1]

The beheading sword was a heavy, two-handed weapon, the proper use of which required great skill and strength; for the victim's stance, and the fact that he was not bound, gave him freedom of motion; and naturally he often flinched before the stroke. There are only too many records of executions at which criminals were merely wounded by the first blow, or refused to stand up to receive it, whereupon the proceedings became a revolting butchery. Such scenes angered the spectators, who

[1] On the central buttress of the Great Hall of the Nuremburg Rathaus is a mural painting dated 1613. It represents an execution by means of a primitive guillotine, but this method did not apparently find favour.

applauded neat workmanship. Once an artist beheaded two felons with a single stroke, a feat that delighted the onlookers.

Beheading ranked, relatively speaking, as an honourable end. Hanging was considered disgraceful and was usually reserved for thieves and criminals of low birth. The substitution of the sword for the halter was considered a favour in such cases. This happened in 1609, out of regard for the felon's two daughters, who complained that their betrothed would refuse to marry the children of one who had been hanged. On another occasion the same indulgence was shown to a thief, on the grounds that he had not benefited by his theft.

Except for very outrageous crimes women were not hanged, but beheaded.

Should the rope break, or any hitch occur, the victim received no mercy, but was again suspended till he was dead.

The halter originally used was, as at one time in Scotland and in Ireland, made of withies. Later, hemp or a chain, or both in conjunction, were employed.

Sometimes prisoners were garotted ; two

men condemned to death by burning were, as an act of grace, so strangled before the fire was lit ; and the same method was often used to mitigate the agony of those sentenced to death by impaling, burying alive or breaking on the wheel, a punishment chiefly reserved for murderers. The offender was bound to a wheel, after which his limbs were broken by blows with a sharp-edged bar, so that the victim was almost hacked to pieces. Forty was the regulation number of strokes ; the last, and fatal one, being delivered on the breast over the heart or on the nape of the neck. So hideous was the spectacle that it seems to have been too much even for the brutal mobs of the time ; therefore the executioner, acting on secret orders, usually hastened to deal the finishing blow. In the case of Schmidt's brother-in-law, however, no less than thirty-one strokes were inflicted.

The wheel itself rested on a tripod, the top of which passed through the nave. This support varied from three to several feet in height, and the blows were delivered either downwards or upwards accordingly.

Burning to death was the punishment for murderers, robbers, coiners, heretics, wizards suspected of dealing in poisons, and those guilty of unnatural sexual crime. In the latter instance, if an animal was involved, it was burnt along with the criminal. Often, however, felons condemned to the fire were previously strangled, beheaded, or drowned. It was also usual to cast a coiner's or a wizard's implements, or a heretic's books, on the same pyre that consumed the offender; and, as a mark of infamy, the bodies of suicides were either burnt or put into a cask and flung into the river.

Horrible as were these punishments, they were not the worst inflicted. In 1392 a man who had murdered his mother is said to have been boiled to death in a cauldron of oil ; and till 1513 some criminals, and the majority of adulterous women, were buried alive ; but in that year, because of the dreadful scenes witnessed at an execution of this kind, drowning replaced it as a punishment, for which method beheading was afterwards substituted when women were concerned.

Drowning was carried out near the Haller-wiese. A wooden stage was built over the Pegnitz, and from it the felon, enclosed in a sack, was thrown into the river and kept below the surface by means of a pole that the *Löwe* handled. One poor wretch contrived to free herself from the sack, and swam, imploring for mercy, but was not reprieved, though her death struggles lasted almost a full hour. The horror of this execution induced the Council, by Schmidt's advice, to abolish this method of punishment in favour of beheading when women were to be the sufferers.

Quartering was inflicted on traitors, whose remains were exhibited on the City gates. The heads of women executed for child murder were nailed above the gallows.

As an aggravation of the death penalty, impaling was practised, especially on those who were buried alive, although this method was really an act of mercy in such cases. Another form of severity was the nipping of victims with red-hot tongs on their way to death. In one instance the executioner refused to give more than four nips ; but Master Schmidt received, and scrupulously carried out, the command to employ this torture without mercy on stubborn or gross criminals. Such was not the only use of the instrument, for with it a blasphemer's tongue was torn out, to be exhibited on the Ohrenstock near the Fleischbrücke.

Jews were not only hanged from a special beam, but a cap lined with hot pitch was also placed on their heads before they swung. It was customary to hang a dog alongside such criminals. One Jewish felon had been condemned to hang by the feet till he was dead, but was graciously spared this punishment and strung up in a Christian fashion.

Death sentences were not always carried out. It occasionally happened that some extenuating circumstances moved the authorities to mercy. By way of warning, the sufferer was made to endure the agony of the full preparations, and respited at the last moment, when the noose already encircled his neck, or when the sword was swung aloft.

Among extenuating circumstances were reckoned the following: (a) extreme youth, (*b*) the fact that the crime had been committed in self defence. In early times the latter reason sufficed for a full acquittal, and in the case of a criminal who was so pardoned at the last moment his accuser angrily declared that justice was no longer to be had in Nuremberg. It is extraordinary to find that a thief escaped the noose on the plea that he had not been able to enjoy the proceeds of his crime. One murderer was reprieved through the representations of thirty peasants. He was, however, drawn thrice round the gibbet on a sledge (or hurdle) before he was released.

Accomplices found to be less guilty than the principal were compelled, as a warning, to witness his execution. Morbid curiosity often lured undetected rogues to haunt the gallows when a criminal was to suffer. One law-breaker, having mingled with the crowd to witness the end of a confederate, was detected by the latter, who in an unsportsmanlike fashion denounced him. The incautious sensation-seeker was thereupon arrested, tried, condemned, and executed.

Avowals of guilt were usually extracted by

threats or by torture, and recantations were common, especially on the scaffold, but never effected their purpose.

Criminals met death in various ways, and of these many interesting details are noted by Schmidt. Often a crowd of sympathisers gathered round the gallows, and on the occasion of a dreadful execution, when a gypsy man was broken on the wheel, the sinister instrument was decorated with flowers by the victim's sweetheart.

Although such spectacles were intended to act as deterrents they utterly failed to do so. It was, even in early times, a matter of comment that those who perished on the scaffold had been among the most regular spectators at such performances. The brutal mobs enjoyed these exhibitions, which frequently gave rise to scenes of coarse revelry and debauch among the onlookers. Drinking and eating booths were set up for the occasion, and the stall-holders paid heavy rent to the Council for these pitches. So great were the crowds at times that two hundred wagon loads of victuals were found to be barely sufficient to feed the spectators. Occasionally the City gates were closed in order to limit the concourse.

The bodies of those condemned to hanging were allowed to swing till they rotted or were devoured by carrion birds. Of those who were beheaded, some found a resting place in the burial plot of St. Peter's church, which lay outside the walls not far from the Hochgericht. The corpses of criminals were usually disposed of in unhallowed ground ; many were thrown into the Pegnitz river, others burnt. In later times dead felons were frequently handed over for dissection to hospitals, or to the hangman, who sold parts of the corpse very profitably to the superstitious, as has already been mentioned. It would also appear that sick people sometimes bribed the *Hochrichter* to allow them to drink the blood streaming from the trunk of the newly beheaded. Bodies left on the gibbet were often robbed of their clothing by ghoulish ruffians, who also stole severed heads, or cut off hands, fingers, feet, etc., to sell or use as charms.

Not content with official executions the Council had recourse to questionable methods for the destruction of law-breakers. In 1408 leave was given to anyone to murder a certain enemy of the State, within a fixed period. In 1536, with the sanction of the authorities, a woman was stoned to death by the mob. Again, in 1611 a traitor and his wife were killed by their own apprentices ; and this summary act of justice was approved by the Council.

The mob indeed required little encouragement to cruelty ; those who were condemned to banishment often suffered terribly at the hands of spectators when the criminal was escorted beyond the boundaries, nor did the Government endeavour to check outbreaks of this nature. How cruel were the times is shown by the following incident. The mother of two executed thieves was, as one privy to their doings, publicly flogged. After this sentence had been carried out, the crowd fell upon her, beat her unmercifully, dragged her to the gallows in order that she should " look at her spawn," and finally so maltreated her that she was left for dead in a ditch near the execution ground.

In so brief an outline it has not been possible to do more than touch on the chief features of the criminal procedure and punishments enacted by the Nuremberg Code. The mass of information available is large, and in many points obscure. Schmidt's diary supplies little information as to legal procedure, or as to the details of executions, but it contains much interesting matter relating to the careers of his victims, with occasional vivid and terse descriptions of the manner in which the condemned met their fate.

A document of great value to students of German criminology is the *Lochordnung*, an anonymous ballad composed by a jail-bird about the beginning of the sixteenth century. It consists of more than one hundred rhyming couplets, rough, iambic tetrameters, and with grim humour as well as pathos describes a felon's progress from the *Loch* to the gallows. The Head Jailer is a genial host, but his guests must pay with their life for such hospitality. As for the beds, they are well enough ; there are pillows and a bolster, but no sheets, and the only covering is a rough pelt. The author's offence is merely that he has stolen washing from a line, yet the owners thirst for his life.

The Head Jailer takes his new guest to a small room, and treacherously advises him to speak the truth as the surest way of escaping the worst. The Council will examine the prisoner after a meal. This the prison maidservant brings to the offender, but the latter complains that he must eat his food off the cover of the foul smelling sanitary tub in his cell. When the felon has fed, the *Lochhüter* again visits him, and after once more exhorting him to confess, leads him to a small room where two members of the Council are seated, along with the prison clerk, who takes down minutes of the proceedings.

The two examiners benignly exhort the accused to confess ; if he refuses the executioner and the *Löwe* enter, clothe the felon in a white smock and hose, and lead him to the Folterkammer, where he is racked with various instruments. The *Löwe* in particular is busy with the windlass, by means of which the punishment of the *stein* was inflicted. A short respite is allowed between the application of the different tortures. The author states that the *Löwe* is then bidden to find two honourable men who shall bear witness to the proceedings and to the confession (a method that by the beginning of the sixteenth century had replaced the ancient practice of the *Ubersiebnen*).

The prisoner is then removed to the condemned cell, and heavily ironed. Here two officials interview him, and in a genial and kindly fashion warn him that he has proved himself worthy of death. Let him therefore prepare to die decently, and attend to his soul's welfare. Good meals are now allowed him, even, as the author grimly remarks, if famine prevails in Nuremberg. The two prison chaplains minister to him : he is, if repentant, allowed the sacrament, and day and night warders keep him under surveillance lest he should attempt to cheat the gallows.

Finally, clothed in a black garment, he is brought to the Judgment Hall, where his crime is loudly proclaimed, and the Honourable Council pronounce his doom. He pleads that he may die by the sword, and the request is mercifully granted. After this he is led down to the entrance of the jail, whence, preceded by two armed riders and with a chaplain on either hand, he is conducted outside the City gate to the place of execution. Here the executioner beheads him, the corpse is sewn up in a winding sheet and laid in the burial ground of St. Peter's church.

THE PROCESSION FROM THE TOWN HALL TO THE GALLOWS

VI. FRANZ SCHMIDT'S DIARY

WITH regard to the Diary itself, as many of the entries are little more than bare and monotonous records of executions and punishments, only those have been selected which offer any interest, or cast light on the criminal procedure of Nuremberg.

These remarks apply peculiarly to the Second Part. The entries in it are limited to minor chastisements carried out by Schmidt and his *Löwe*. Apparently the hangman did not consider most of them worthy of elaboration, for the vast majority of these items merely state the name of the condemned, the offence, and the punishment inflicted, with here and there a note that the rogue was afterwards executed.

The meagre nature of these entries gives us little clue as to why some criminals escaped the gallows and worse punishments, to which others, seemingly no more guilty, were sentenced. In their decisions the Nuremberg

Council must have been guided by the consideration of facts unknown to us.

Out of the 345 convicted people mentioned in this section, about 300 were merely whipped and banished. Some fifteen were mutilated, generally by the loss of fingers; a few by that of a hand or of the ears. Less than ten seem to have been pilloried; a small number were clapped in the stocks; a couple suffered branding; and two were condemned to banishment without the whipping that usually accompanied this penalty. Occasionally two or more of these punishments were combined; but considering the times the record is one of comparative mildness. Of the criminals who suffered bodily punishment, approximately eight per cent. were, according to Schmidt, afterwards executed, mostly by hanging.

An attempt has been made to follow Schmidt closely, and where we have his own words this is as a rule fairly simple; but as Herr Keller points out, bad copying and interpolations have in places grossly, sometimes almost hopelessly, corrupted the text. Such portions cannot be translated without conjecturing some missing links. Fortunately these are almost always unimportant and do not affect the historic value of the record. We have followed Schmidt's somewhat erratic spelling of the names, both of persons and places.

For assistance in composing the summary large use has been made of Dr. Hermann Knapp's *Nürnberger Kriminal Recht*, 1896 ; as well as of the same author's *Der Lochgefängniss, Tortur, und Richtung in Alt-Nürnberg*, 1907 ; both very learned and able expositions of a most difficult subject. We gladly take this opportunity of expressing our indebtedness to these works, which, together with the *Zeitschrift für Kulturgeschichte* and other publications, have been of the greatest help.

Lastly, we wish to express our grateful thanks to Dr. A. Altmann, Archivdirektor of the Bayerisches Staatsarchiv, Nuremberg, for the trouble which he has been to in searching out and procuring for us the illustrations that adorn this book, and also for answering several queries.

INTRODUCTION TO SCHMIDT'S DIARY

by
ALBRECHT KELLER

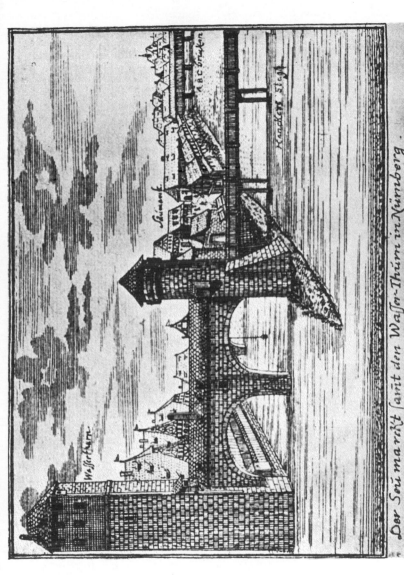

Der Seü marckt sanīt den Wasser-Thürn in Nürnberg.

THE HANGMAN'S BRIDGE (HENKERSTEG), NUREMBERG

FROM AN ENGRAVING, *circa* BEGINNING OF 17TH CENTURY. TOWN LIBRARY AT NUREMBERG

(*The tower in the middle of the picture, and the portion of the bridge adjoining it on the left, were,*
at that time, assigned to the executioner as a residence)   (*face p.* 75)

INTRODUCTION TO SCHMIDT'S DIARY

OVER the two stone arches of the Hangman's Bridge in Nuremberg the executioner used to pass from his home on the island to his bloody work on the Raven's Stone—the place of execution—before the Virgin's Gate.

To this day, the roofed bridge with the massive Water Tower beside it is one of the most picturesque and impressive corners in a town abounding in memories of olden times. It stands hard by the romantic splendour of pointed roof and gable, a sombre picture from the dark side of life in the Middle Ages, testifying to the profound contrast between the overflowing joy of life of the citizens and the pitiless severity with which they protected themselves and their possessions against the 'dangerous people' who gazed up at the lofty houses with envious eyes.

Like all old German towns, Nuremberg, 'that German town full of noble arts,' had frequent recourse to the arm of the dour, hardened headsman. The city of Albrecht Dürer and honest Hans Sachs was no more cruel nor inhuman than any other community possessing its own judicial powers over life and death. The ' Iron Maiden ' in the Torture Chamber of the Castle is a gross fiction ; the chroniclers make no mention of this idle invention of a morbid imagination. And with the exception of Frankfort-on-Main, Nuremberg was the only German town where witch hunting never assumed the proportions of a contagious popular malady, burning itself out only with the embers of the last glowing faggot. It is true that occasionally a man or woman fell into the executioner's hands on a charge of sorcery, but the Nuremberg Council, as they stated in a letter written to Ulm in 1531, never believed in witches and therefore ' took no other measures against such persons than to banish them from their territory.' When seventy-two witches were hanged or burnt in the neighbouring town of Ellingen in 1591, the Nuremberg Council, despite great popular indignation, forbade the torture of an old woman accused of witchcraft, and ordained that no criminal process should be set in motion against persons accused on mere report ; and that any authority so offending should be held liable to be called to account by the accused party for injury, and be cast in costs and damages. An executioner's assistant who tried to cast suspicion of sorcery on the wives of certain citizens was incontinently beheaded.

The popular imagination, therefore, which seeks to associate the Hangman's Bridge with all kinds of sanguinary horrors, is as mistaken in this respect as it is regarding the ' Iron Maiden.' What the Nuremberg executioner did in the course of his duty was no more horrible in itself than what our modern executioner, whom our own age also deems indispensable, has to perform. The only difference is that the services of the former were more frequently required and for purposes other than execution alone.

The executioner of Nuremberg, Franz Schmidt, has himself informed us what his duties were, for he has left us a detailed diary of all his executions. Franz Schmidt is not the only ' author ' amongst men of his calling. In the introduction to the hangmen's novels of

Julius von der Traun (Berlin, Mayer & Jessen, 1911) Alfred von Berger mentions the diary of the executioner at Salzburg, and a wider circle of readers is acquainted with Karl Huss, the executioner of Eger, whom Goethe, in his travels to the Spa at Karlsbad, often visited, in order to examine his remarkable collections ; his book on superstitions, composed in 1823, has been edited by Alois John.

Franz Schmidt narrates the gruesome duties of his office. It is a singular book, fascinating and, at the same time, horrible ; no book for weaklings to read, yet true and genuine as only a personal document can be. The edition published in 1801 by J. M. F. von Endter has long been out of print and is only rarely to be found in collectors' catalogues ; the extract included by Christian Meyer in the seventh volume of the Hohenzollern Researches (1902) could be expected to appeal only to a limited circle of readers. There is, therefore, some justification for a new edition that will render the bloody life-task of the executioner accessible as an original source for the study of the growth of civilisation and legal history, despite the horror of the contents.

In the first place, the Diary brings clearly and vividly before our eyes the legal system of the waning Middle Ages ; its pages are filled with everything that occupied the criminal courts of the sixteenth and seventeenth centuries. Here are no exceptional cases, no collection of judgments of merely local interest ; what happened in Nuremberg could occur in any other mediæval town. And yet it is a narrative of the most dreadful crimes, which follow each other in horrible succession, crimes which must be atoned for by blood and torture ; a record of cruel murderers and highway robbers, of youthful thieves and relapsed criminals, of coiners, incendiaries, forgers and poisoners, of swindlers and treasure seekers, who know how to exploit the superstitions of their fellow creatures ; of infanticides and betrayed women ; the unfortunate and the criminal pass before our eyes in a ghastly procession. Even the *cause célèbre* is not lacking : the advocate and counsellor, whom years of fraud and incest bring at last to the Sword of Justice.

All of them are overtaken by the punishment they have earned : the gallows for the thief, the sword and the wheel for the slayer and murderer, the stake and flames for the incendiary, the coiner and those guilty of unnatural vice. The old principle of the *lex talionis* still survives : eye for eye, tooth for tooth ; the ' dooms ' of Germanic law are based on that principle. The perjurer loses his finger, the blasphemer his tongue, or the tip of his tongue. And, as in the remotest times, the execution is carried out in public ; it is intended to be a deterrent. The thief makes atonement for his secret crime by being forced in the eyes of the multitude to ' peep through the hempen noose,' or ' ride the gallows-tree,' or however the thieves' slang of the day might be pleased to express it. Therefore the linen bleachers provide a white dress for the linen stealer to wear on his last journey to the gallows. The corpse remains hanging from the gallows until it rots away, so that the rogue who travels the highway may have a warning example. It is for this reason that the place of execution was visible from afar, and was an object of pride to the community which vaunted the possession of legal powers over life and death and the vigorous execution of its justice. For that reason also no Jew might swing from the gallows : a projecting beam was good enough for him ; in earlier times a hatful of melted pitch was emptied over his head—if indeed he were not strung up by his legs. Even the penalty of flogging for lesser thieves and rogues, and for the vagrant wenches of the woods, was intended to ensure a keener remembrance and more salutary dread.

Far removed from the humane feelings of the present day, which maintains the enemies of society at the expense of the community, recourse was had to severe and bloody punishments in order to get rid of harmful folk in a cheap and easy fashion. This is the reason why so many of these crimes, which appear to modern sentiment as petty delinquencies, were punished with such severity. The power of the Nuremberg law did not extend very far : whoever was not caught *flagrante delicto* could put the boundaries behind him in a few hours, and therefore it is easy to understand that relatively few criminals met with their deserts, however much the courts of law of various towns played into each other's hands. A delinquent who was caught received such a memento that for the future he would keep well out of the way. A mutilated hand was the sign-manual of an oath-breaker : the significance of the letter N branded on both cheeks was obvious to all, and anyone who had been flogged out of the town at the cart's tail had had enough of Nuremberg. So at least it seemed to the public opinion of the day. For a flogging of that kind, the first introduction to the public hangman, was no trivial matter ; many died of its effects. The habitual thief and rogue, however, received short shrift. If such individuals were not sent to the galleys for a number of years under the terms of a treaty made with Genoa—a form of punishment which, like the banishment to prisons on the Hungarian border, was soon suspended owing to the great expense entailed —their last hour had struck ; and it was considered an act of grace if they were permitted to escape the shameful gallows and fall instead by the more honourable sword.

It must be admitted that the penal code of Nuremberg was Draconian: society was to be kept morally pure, even if the sternest forms of compulsion had to be applied. Therefore wenches were made to confess the names of all the men with whom they had had relations, and any butcher who sold the flesh of dogs for human consumption was sent to the gallows.

Criminal procedure can also be ascertained from the Diary. We hear of the prison-hole in the cellars of the old Town Hall, where the prisoner in danger of the gallows was interrogated by the magistrates. If 'kindly persuasion' had no result, torture, graduated to extract a confession, awaited him. For, ever since Roman law with its process by inquisition had supplanted the old German procedure of conviction obtained by the evidence of witnesses, every effort was made to obtain a confession, without which no sentence could be passed. Thus the accused became his own accuser. On one occasion a man was beheaded in Nuremberg, who confessed to a murder, although the corpse of the victim could not be discovered in the place indicated by him.

The ancient form of ' ordeal of the bier,' at which it was supposed that the murdered man's blood would flow afresh at the touch of the murderer, the strongest proof by means of circumstantial evidence, was no longer suited to this conception of law. It is mentioned only once in Schmidt's diary, and in this instance the accused woman was actually pardoned, although the spot of blood on the body of the little victim was sufficient evidence of her guilt.

When the accused had confessed he was formally sentenced in open court.

The old jurisprudence punished not only the act but its consequences. Whoso therefore had been unable to enjoy the fruits of his misdeeds, got off more cheaply. But the day was still far distant when crime would be judged in its relationship to the moral state of the criminal. The youthful age of an offender was seldom regarded as an extenuating circumstance, and never in the case of incorrigible thieves. In the year 1574 Franz Schmidt's predecessor in Nuremberg hanged three children, none of whom was more than fourteen years old ;

on another occasion, as Schmidt himself relates, five young fellows were ' all hanged from one beam.' In the year 1575, six wicked lads who had all forfeited their lives by repeated robberies, fell into the hands of the Council of Nuremberg ; but as they were too young for the gallows, the five youngest, with hands tied behind their backs and with halters round their necks, were exhibited on the scaffold on three successive days, and in addition were daily chastised with rods by the *Löwe* (the title of the executioner's assistant) in their prison. On February the 3rd the eldest, eighteen years of age (another account says fifteen years), was hanged ; the five others were chained together, led before him, and placed at the foot of the ladder on the scaffold where they could get a good view of him, and were then banished. The ages of the five young thieves were only nine to eleven years ! In the year 1584 a thirteen-year-old boy was hanged. The murderer who on April 28th, 1579, was torn with red-hot pincers and then broken on the wheel, was only eighteen years old.

That human society itself possibly bore a

share in the guilt of such a squandering of youthful life ; that perhaps many a man became bad simply because he was called bad ; such ideas never entered the heads of any of the severe Councillors who condemned youths to death or cast them out on to the highways, where they were effectually set on the path which led to a dreadful end on the gallows.

Drunkenness was an extenuating circumstance only in so far as the security of public life was not endangered by a pardon. And therefore a master craftsman who in a drunken revel had stabbed a prostitute to death in the public street had to pay the penalty with his life, although the woman had given him the utmost provocation ; for he had already committed a similar crime under similar conditions.

Infanticide was punished with merciless severity. No consideration was taken of the misery of the betrayed mother who found herself abandoned to infamy without any hope of escape save by ridding herself of the offspring of her sin. But even worse than the heavy penalty was the circumstance that, of all the gaping multitued who crowded round the place of execution, none felt the monstrousness of the sentence. The death penalty was a matter of course that troubled the consciences of none of them, whereas the man who, as seducer, was after all the co-partner in guilt, was merely banished. It is true that the ' poor sinner,' like all other ' poor sinners,' was sure of universal pity ; but as Hebbel says, ' Pity is the cheapest of all human sentiments.' It was the authority of the Church that laid such special stress on the sanctity of the newly born infant's life. According to the celebrated Karolina Criminal Code of the Emperor Charles V, a woman guilty of infanticide was to be buried alive or impaled, and the penalty of death by drowning was to be inflicted only where ' water for the purpose was conveniently at hand.' A great reform, therefore, was brought about by Franz Schmidt when, in the year 1580, he succeeded in securing for these poor creatures the penalty of death by beheading, a reform that might easily have prejudiced his professional reputation, since, as was pointed out to him, ' these females through timidity might fall to the ground and thus obliged to finish them off as they lay prone on the earth.'

It might at first sight appear that perjury was punished more leniently; but what Franz Schmidt and the old law called perjury is not perjury in the modern meaning of the word. The procedure by torture had no need of sworn witnesses, since its object was to force the accused to make confession of his guilt, and it was thought that torture was a better means of finding out the truth. In Schmidt's diary the meaning of the word is always the breach of the oath to keep the peace which every condemned person was compelled to swear, namely that he would never take vengeance for that which he had suffered, and everyone who was banished from the town had to swear that he would never return. The rod inflicted an appropriate punishment on those who broke their sworn promise. That was the best way of dealing with the skulking rabble of the streets and the woods.

Flogging out of the town was the penalty for bigamy and polygamy, the remarkably frequent occurrence of which can be accounted for only by the ease with which, through the whole of the

THE FRAUENTOR

FROM A PEN-AND-INK DRAWING MADE *circa* BEGINNING OF 17TH CENTURY
TOWN LIBRARY AT NUREMBERG

(*face p.* 88)

seventeenth century, marriage could be contracted. Nothing more was required than the promise of marriage ; there were no witnesses, no publication of banns from the pulpit, in spite of all the efforts of the authorities, lay and clerical, to suppress such 'hole and corner marriages.' Whereas the Karolina Code insisted on the death penalty for bigamy, 'which is not merely a breach of the marriage vow but is also greater than this latter crime,' the mild view of Nuremberg gradually contented itself with inflicting the rod. In earlier times the penalty had been death by drowning.

Mechanically as this interpretation of the law clung to the Code, we are deeply moved to find that the poor sinner was sometimes pardoned, even on the scaffold, in complete violation and suspension of the usual course of procedure, in Nuremberg and elsewhere. Franz Schmidt mentions several cases of this kind, though unfortunately without stating who secured this mitigation. We find no mention in his book of any romantic betrothal on the scaffold, although this was not altogether unknown. In 1525 the executioner of Rotenburg, who had been called in as an assistant, demanded in marriage the female infanticide whom he was to execute.

From the end of the sixteenth century the Council at Nuremberg almost invariably passed sentence of beheading by the sword as the mode of carrying the death penalty into effect, whilst the severer forms of execution and the horrible mutilations were inflicted only in rare instances. The Bamberg sequel to the Diary often mentions that the poor sinners whose sentences had been commuted from the gallows to the sword as an act of favour ' thanked the magistrates for their clemency and bade them farewell.' The sentence of burning was carried out only after the criminals had been strangled, though the strangling of Georg Karl Lamprecht, the last person to be executed by Franz Schmidt, was bungled, so that the unfortunate man was in fact burnt alive.

How great were the brutality and indifference which could maintain the strict application of the dread death penalty, and could find it quite natural that every few days, year after year, some man or woman should be lashed through the streets with bleeding backs, and that every few weeks some wretch should quiver under the sword of the executioner! Of such little account was human life that the theft of bees was regarded as a crime worthy of death.

When a poor sinner was led out to die, a whole concourse of persons, young and old, followed, and especially " the inquisitive females who love to gape at everything." The populace crowded together in such numbers that often the town gates had to be shut in order to maintain order. Yet would it be otherwise in our own day, if we were to regard an execution as a popular entertainment ? The reason for it all was the idea that a public execution had a deterrent effect, and to none of the sage Councillors did it occur that crime did not diminish, but that the executioner continued his task, as his predecessors had done for centuries.

According to his own computation, Franz Schmidt carried out nearly four hundred executions in his forty-three years of office, and he has either forgotten to record many cases, or they were carried out by the *Löwe*, his assistant.

Brief and to the point are his entries in the register of his bloody work.

The legal historian will find many *lacunæ* in this Diary. The limited education of the executioner, who evidently wrote down his impressions immediately after each execution, is the cause of much confusion. He had not the same mastery over the pen as he had over his sword. Indeed, it is remarkable enough that he was able to read and write at all. But his education was not sufficient for him to arrange his thoughts in orderly sequence, and therefore innumerable legal cases are only partly comprehensible, and others not at all. Those who desire to study any particular case will perhaps be able to fill in the gaps by consulting the many other chronicles, protocols, and criminal registers which Nuremberg still possesses. The records of Hagedorn, the Ordinary of St. Sibald, who was entrusted with the charge of giving ghostly comfort to the poor sinners, are still in existence. Our present source of legal information seems defective simply because all the trials that ended with an acquittal or bloodless punishment are naturally omitted ; for the executioner does not register cases in which his services were not required. It is just this limitation of the record to cases where life and limb actually suffered that makes the Diary a veritable book of blood.

Workers in other branches of knowledge can derive profit from the book, especially the student of nomenclature. Every person who passes through his hands is registered by Schmidt under his supposed baptismal name as well as under the nickname by which he was popularly known in the town. He has compiled a whole catalogue of names of criminals in his record of the associates of the two robbers and murderers who were executed in 1593. The executioner does not appear to have known that the Councillor Nicholas von Gülchen who was beheaded in 1605 was really called Nicholas Weber. The family name was still used only in official intercourse, and it was by the name of his birthplace that the people referred to the distinguished gentleman who had come to live amongst them.

And what a wealth of minute and precious

detail does the Diary offer, particularly in the realm of social history! The soul of the Middle Ages is laid bare before us. Here a young girl hopes to fetter the affections of a youth by a love potion, there a woman seeks to make her man invulnerable, even proof against torture, so that he shall utter no confession. Everywhere mysterious powers, which can be turned to advantage, are deemed to be latent, even in the genital organs of thieves, and especially in the fingers of unborn male babes. Schmidt repeatedly mentions how atrocious murderers obtained thieves' candles of that material. And amusing traits are revealed amongst much that is horrible. A merry farce of Hans Sachs lives again when a rogue professes to have come from the Venusberg. And that cunning shepherd, who for years had been playing the ghost in order to visit the farmer's daughter undisturbed, would furnish the stuff for a true comedy. Then again there are gruesome pictures from the life of the people : a gaping woman recognises her husband in the poor sinner who is faring on his last journey in this world, and to whom she bids a

weeping farewell. Another time we are over-
come with the gruesome mood of a folk-song,
such as might form part of the collection *Des
Knaben Wunderhorn* when we are told of pretty
Anna, who was murdered and robbed in the
wood on her way to her betrothed.

And then again it is strange to read in what
frame of mind the poor sinner goes to his doom :
one mounts the gallows' ladder ' impudently
and waggishly,' perhaps even still cracking his
scurrilous jests ; a second, after all sorts of
useless remonstrances, resigns himself to his
fate ; a third is almost beside himself with
grief. Even for the skilled executioner it was
no light task to behead swiftly and surely a
victim so completely broken down. How easy
it was to make a mis-hit ! Such was the experi-
ence of Franz Schmidt ; the manuscript of the
Germanic National Museum indicates in several
places that he had bungled the execution.
Quite apart from the disgrace, such a mishap
might easily become a serious matter for the
executioner : the people frequently took the
part of the now doubly unfortunate sinner. In
the year 1641 Franz Schmidt's second successor,

Valentin Deusser, was discharged from his post
' on account of his slovenly workmanship ' ;
he had the misfortune to miss the poor woman,
so that she fell down twice from the chair ;
and on his way home he would have been stoned
to death, if the town guard had not come to his
help in the nick of time ![1]   A double execution
on June 27th, 1665, passed off still worse :
' The woman Wörner was clumsily executed,
for after five strokes she still cried out, and
finally her head was taken off as she lay on the
Raven's Stone ; the man Merckel had also 25

---

[1] The Bamberg M.S. says of this gruesome execution:
' This poor sinner was very ill and weak, so that she had to
be led to the Krippelstein, and when she had sat down upon
the chair, Master Valtin, the hangman, walked round her like
a cat round a hot broth and held the sword a span from her
neck, and took aim and then struck the blow and missed her
neck and struck off a piece of her head as big as a dollar and
struck her down from the chair.   Then the poor soul got up
quicker than she had sat down, and this blow did not harm
her.   Then she began to beg that she should be allowed to go,
because she had been so brave; but all in vain; and she had
to sit down again.   Then the Löwe (the assistant) wanted to
take the sword from Master Valtin and strike with it himself; but this the master would not allow, and himself struck
a second blow somewhat stronger, so that she again fell to
the ground, and then he cut off her head as she lay upon the
scaffold.   Whereupon he, the hangman, had his reward as
he went home; for he would soon have been stoned to death
if the armed town guard had not rescued him, inasmuch as
the blood was already streaming from his head.'

strokes given to him on the wheel, after which he still stirred, and because the executioner killed these two poor wretches so clumsily, he was discharged from his post, and these were the last persons whom he executed.'

Hanging, too, was not so simple, as Franz Schmidt's successor was to learn on February 1st, 1620. 'The criminal died a bitter, slow death on the gallows. He was the first whom Master Bernard Schlegel, the executioner of this town, had hanged. Master Bernard tortured the victim severely, seated himself astride the gallows, called the name Jesus thrice overloud in his ears, took him by the hair of his head, and pressed him down often with all his strength and handled him most unmercifully until he choked him. A double ladder of new oak had been made for him for this his first execution, which however was not successful, for everybody was disgusted with his manner of hanging, abused him, cursed him, and wished him every ill, so that he was like to have been stoned had the crowd been able to loosen the hard frozen clods of earth.'

But the chronicles also mention the masterpieces of the executioner: 'On October 20th,

1645, Matthias Perger took off head and both hands at one blow.'

Apparently it was never made a cause of complaint against Franz Schmidt by the Council that he occasionally had bad luck. He gives us the impression of a man held in esteem, if one can use that term about a person who was shunned by his fellow townsfolk. He maintained a just mind and moral earnestness despite the bloody nature of his craft, despite the rigour with which he applied the torture, and despite the cruel severity—or was it lack of skill?—with which in 1585 he gave the finishing blow to his own brother-in-law only after the thirty-first stroke on the wheel.

Schmidt never took wine or other strong drink. It is true that he regards human beings, from his own special point of view, as good or bad subjects for his professional skill. But he relates with pride, how with the help of two priests he succeeded in having the death penalty for women guilty of infanticide changed from drowning to decapitation. And Knapp is perhaps correct in his conjecture that the

sane ideas of the executioner helped to prevent
the practice of witch hunting from taking root
in Nuremberg ; for it is only too well known
how greatly this dreadful frenzy was furthered
by those who exploited it for their own ends.
Not that Franz Schmidt disbelieved in witches :
the executioner would be the very first person
likely to fall a victim to a belief in black
magic and sorcery.   Moreover, though 'void of
honour,' he knew that his task was a necessary
one and that it had its own standard of honour,
and in the secure feeling of duty faithfully
performed he looked down with disdain upon
the criminals, ' these gallowbirds,' who were
delivered into his hands.   As an honourable
man he made a mark of approval in his register
of blood whenever a criminal had behaved
well and had made a Christian end.   Only a
man thoroughly convinced of the importance
of his office would hit upon the idea of giving
a written account of it.   Feared by all evildoers
as master of life and death, shunned by all
others with dread, he was yet sought out in the
darkness of night and consulted as the holder
of valuable secrets and as a skilled surgeon

possessing a more profound knowledge of the
human body (so often ' adonomised ' by him)
than most physicians of his time, and as one
who could do more than merely reduce the
racked and dislocated joints of his unfortunate
victims. Every executioner bequeathed his
knowledge and his calling to his son, whom
the heartless prejudice of human society obliged
to adopt the same office. He regarded himself
as a benefactor of mankind who with his sure
sword shears through a life that, perhaps for
years, has terrorised a whole district, and this
is something, he thinks, which is certainly
worthy to be chronicled.

And what a vigorous, pithy style the man
has! One feels how difficult the executioner
finds the task of forcing the pen to obey his
hand. His style is short and sharp like his
swordsmanship, each word weighty and incisive.
Of literary construction, whether grammatical
or logical, he has scant knowledge : in one
breath he relates that a ' fellow has taken
5 guilders and three wives.' Many a deed
which he avenged with a violent death seems
to us a judicial murder simply because in his

honest indignation he has forgotten to inform us of the most important facts.

Franz Schmidt died in 1634, having resigned his office previously, and was buried ' honourably.'

.   .   .   .

The original Diary is lost, and in its place we possess four manuscripts and one printed copy.

The oldest manuscript, that in the Germanic National Museum in Nuremberg, belongs to about the middle of the seventeenth century. It is neat, and carefully written, without any corrections, as is the second which dates from the commencement of the nineteenth century and is in the possession of the Municipal Library at Nuremberg. Both agree in their text to the smallest details, though frequently the more modern form of speech has crept into the more recent version. They both break off their narrative of the executions with No. 287, and thus give an additional proof of their close relationship. On the other hand the manuscript which was formerly kept at the Castle in Nuremberg and which was used by von Endter as the basis of his edition, is complete. Undoubtedly this version has been less carefully transcribed, numerous sentences have been omitted, and many words have been mis-read or misunderstood.

Against the three manuscripts in Nuremberg we have to set the two manuscripts that belong to the Royal Library in Bamberg. The first of these can be little older than the manuscript in the Germanic National Museum, the other must be attributed to the second half of the eighteenth century. The former breaks off with the year 1597, but the latter is complete and in addition narrates the executions by Schmidt's successors down to the year 1692. Both have inserted in chronological order amongst the executions the lesser punishments that in the Nuremberg group are catalogued after the executions, and then occasionally a complete *résumé* is added at the end of the year. At the same time both contain the lesser punishments of the year 1591 in the list of 1593, those of 1592 in that of 1594, and those of 1594 in that of 1595, with the remarkable result that according to the manuscript of Bamberg the same Jew was broken on the wheel in 1593 and was flogged out of the town in the following year. In the same year, 1593, two criminals were executed, but their ' widows ' had already been flogged out as early as 1591. Moreover the older manuscript is disfigured by serious mistakes: *adonossirt* is used instead of *adonomirt* *Kebsweib* instead of *Krebsdieb, geboren* instead of *bachen,* and in one passage we are even told that a certain criminal had abducted a rogue (Spitzbuben) as well as a woman. The *Dölpeltaler* has been replaced as being incomprehensible by *Doffeltaler.* For all these reasons the Bamberg manuscripts have no weight in any reconstruction of the text. But they possess a number of short and often valuable additions, which cannot be regarded merely as attempts to continue the monosyllabic style of Franz Schmidt. They contain frequent turns of language which Franz Schmidt has not previously used, such as *Hürlein,* and ' *Einschones Leuth.*' The writer cannot, however, have invented them himself, and therefore the only presumption is that they have been taken from some other source. Such additions, so far as they do not present obvious contradictions, have been inserted in brackets in the present text. Otherwise, the manuscript of the Germanic National Museum has been used as the basis of the text of this edition. Only a simplification of the mode of spelling was necessary. The text even then presents sufficient difficulties.

Herein
All the Executions of
Master Franz
Schmidt Executioner

in Nuremberg; which he carried
out, at first for his Father in this place
and elsewhere; those also when he was
finally appointed by an Honourable Coun=
cil to be executioner of the same Town;
the number of persons, married or single,
whom he executed ; the name of every one;
what each had done ; and what was done
to each, are diligently set forth.

Likewise one may read

of all the bodily punishments, such as
flogging, banishing from the Town, cut=
ting off of fingers and ears, branding of
cheeks, standing in the pillory, and many
other matters.   All to be read, diligently
set forth.   A°1573.

PART I

EXECUTIONS

BEGUN AT BAMBERG
FOR MY FATHER
IN THE YEAR 1573

EXECUTIONS

Year 1573

1. June 5th. Leonhardt Russ, of Ceyern, a thief, hanged at Statt Steinach. Was my first execution.

2. Wolff Weber, of Guntzendorff, and Barthel Dochendte, of Weisterfelss, both executed at Statt Kronach ; Wolff, who was a thief, was hanged ; Barthel, who was a murderer and had committed three murders, was executed on the wheel.

3. Gronla Weygla, of Cleucam, a murderer who had committed five murders with his companions, executed on the wheel at Hollfeld.

4. Barthel Meussel, of Mehrenhüel, a murderer, who single handed committed two murders ; the first at Bamberg at the mill-weir, when he stabbed a man and took his money, the other at Welckendorff on the mountains, when he cut the throat of a man who was sleeping with him on the straw in a shed, and took his

money—beheaded at Hollfeld and exposed on the wheel. This was my first execution with the sword.

Total : 5 persons.

Year 1574

5. A thief hanged.

6. do.

7. Kloss Renckhart of Feylsdorf, a murderer, who committed three murders with an associate. First he shot dead his companion, secondly a miller's man who helped him to attack and plunder a mill by night. The third case was again at a mill, called the Fox Mill, on the mountains, which he attacked at night with a companion. They shot the miller dead, did violence to the miller's wife and the maid, obliged them to fry some eggs in fat and laid these on the dead miller's body, then forced the miller's wife to join in eating them. He kicked the miller's body and said : " Miller, how do you like this morsel ? " He also plundered the mill. For these things he was executed on the wheel at Graytz.

Total : 3 persons.

Year 1575

8. A thief hanged.

9. Wastel Pennas, of Leuchtenberg, a butcher and thief, who also sold dog's flesh as mutton, hanged at Rotkirch.

10. A thief hanged.

Total : 3 persons.

Year 1576

11. A thief hanged.

12. Jacob Nuss, of Hallstatt, who set fire to his own house there, and when his neighbour tried to save it, stabbed him ; beheaded with the sword in the middle of the market-place near the church.

13. A thief hanged.

14. Hans Peyhel, of Forchheim, who committed three murders with his companion ; beheaded with the sword at Forchheim and exposed on the wheel. Two years ago I cut off his ears and flogged him at Herzog Aurach.

15. A thief hanged.

16. do.

17. A murderer beheaded.

18. Nickel Schwager, of Leybskrüen, a mason, who with his companion committed five murders; executed on the wheel at Preseck.

19. Hans Hassen, of Ebing, a tradesman and murderer, who with his brother Kloss committed five murders, executed on the wheel at Forchheim. (*See Part I., No. 27.*)

Total : 9 persons.

Year 1577

20. Hans Weber, of Nuremberg, a thief, hanged here at Nuremberg. This was my first execution here.

21. Two thieves hanged.

22. Nicklauss Stüller, of Aydtsfeld, *alias* Schwartz Kraeker, a murderer. With his companions Phila and Görgla von Sunberg he committed eight murders. First he shot a horse-soldier; secondly he cut open a pregnant woman alive, in whom was a dead child; thirdly he again cut open a pregnant woman in whom was a female child; fourthly he once more cut open a pregnant woman in whom were two male children. Görgla von Sunberg said they

had committed a great sin and that he would take the infants to a priest to be baptized, but Phila said he would himself be priest and baptize them, so he took them by the legs and dashed them to the ground. For these deeds he, Stüller, was drawn out on a sledge at Bamberg, his body torn thrice with red-hot tongs, and then he was executed on the wheel.

23. October 13th. An incendiary beheaded.

24. A thief beheaded as a favour and not hanged.

Total : 6 persons.

Year 1578

25. March 6th. Apollonia Vöglin, of Lehrberg, who murdered a child. She gave birth to an infant at the farm of her master, and killed it ; executed by drowning at Lichtenau.

26. April 10th. Georg Reychl, of Prüge, a furrier and swordsman, a master with the long sword, who stabbed the son of the Teutsche Herr. Beheaded with the sword at Nuremberg.

27. April 15th. Closs Hassn, of Ewingen, a tradesman and a murderer, who with his

brother Hans (already executed) committed five murders at Forcham. Executed on the wheel. (*See Part I., No.* 19.)

This is the beginning of my duties when I, Master Frantz Schmidt, was appointed (executioner) at Nuremberg on St. Walburga's day.

28. Three thieves hanged.

29. July 3rd. Hans Müllner, *alias* der Model, a smith, who violated a girl of thirteen years of age, filling her mouth with sand that she might not cry out; also Hans Kellner of the Reuth by Forchheim, a thief; both beheaded with the sword at Nuremberg.

30. July 21st. Haintz Grossn, *alias* lazy Haintz, a robber, beheaded with the sword at Nuremberg. I dissected and cut up his body.

31. A thief hanged.

32. August 12th. Steffan Hötzelein, *alias* der Lauffenhöltzer, a wire-drawer at Lauff, who accused Georg Schwindel, a councillor there, saying he had seen him commit lewdness with four women; his father, Hans Hötzelein, whose fingers were struck off, bore witness in the matter, the father saying it happened under an oak-tree, the son, on the contrary, under a

fir-tree. The accusation was made through jealousy (which he confessed in prison), he having previously killed a man and also robbed several burghers and women of Lauff of their reputation and honour. Beheaded with the sword at Nuremberg.

33. Two thieves hanged.

The new scaffold was set up at this time.

Total : 13 persons.

Year 1579

34. March 19th. Eberla Eckhardt (a young person) of Nuremberg, a thief, as a favour beheaded standing, with the sword here in Nuremberg.

35. April 28th. George Taucher of Eckels-heim, a murderer who, at three o'clock in the morning, killed a tavern keeper's lad in Pfint-zing's house by the Fruit Market, with a knife he purposely carried about him, cutting his neck and throat—for this crime he was led out on a cart here in Nuremberg, was twice nipped in the arms with red-hot tongs, and then executed on the wheel.

36. May 14th. A murderer beheaded.

37. July 13th. A woman who murdered her illegitimate child ; executed by drowning.

38. August 6th. Hans Büchner of Unterfarrenbach, who had previously been whipped out of the town at Nuremberg, George Gabler of Schönfeld, Michael Dieterich of Pernetswin (*alias* the Margrave), three thieves and robbers, beheaded here with the sword and exposed on the wheel. When they were being led out, the Margrave's wife wanted to see the poor sinners as they passed, and saw her own husband among them, whom she embraced and kissed, for she had not known her husband had been arrested, nor that he was a fellow of that sort.

39. A thief, who was also a cut-purse, hanged.

40. A thief hanged.

41. A murderer beheaded.

42. Two thieves hanged.

Total : 12 persons.

Year 1580

43. January 26th. Margaret Dörfflerin (50 years old) from Ebermannsstatt, Elizabeth

Ernstin (22 years old) from Anspach, Agnes
Lengin (22 years old) of Amberg, three child
murderesses. The woman Dörfflerin, when she
brought forth her child in the garden behind the
Fort, left it lying alive in the snow so that it
froze to death. Ernstin, when she brought
forth her child alive in Master Behcimb's
house, herself crushed its little skull and locked
the body in a trunk. But the woman Lengin,
when she brought forth her child alive in the
house of a smith, throttled it and buried it in
a heap of refuse. All three beheaded with the
sword as murderesses and their heads nailed
above the great scaffold, no woman having
been beheaded before this at Nuremberg. I
and the two priests, namely Master Eucharius
and Master Lienhardt Krieg, brought this about,
as the bridges were already prepared, because
they should all three have been drowned.

44. A robber beheaded.

45. March 3rd. Ulrich Gerstenacker, of Class-
berg, who drove out with his brother to the
wood and slew and murdered him with premeditation, giving out afterwards that the
sledge with the wood had fallen on him and

killed him—brought in here from Betzenstein and beheaded with the sword, then exposed upon the wheel.

46. Two thieves hanged.

47. July 15th. Hans Horn of Korenburg and Wolf Bauer of Rollhofen, *alias* Schnöllgatter, two thieves, George Wigliss, *alias* Habersack of Auerbach, a murderer, who with his companion committed three murders. Two of the victims he killed by surprise, with the help of his companion, in a little wood near Heidelberg, one of them being a barber-surgeon the other a tinman ; the third, whom he killed by himself with a wood-chopper in the Nuremberg Forest near Rötenbach, was a pedlar ; he took 8 florins from him, hung his basket on a tree and covered the body with brushwood. He afterwards took to himself the murdered pedlar's wife at Leinberg, and was married to her. All three executed at Birnbaum, Wigliss on the wheel, the other two with the rope.

48. A horse-thief hanged.

49. Three thieves hanged.

50. August 16th. Margaret Böckin, a citizen of Nuremberg, who murdered another woman,

also a citizen, called 'the Treasurer's wife.' When asked to look for lice, she struck her on the head from behind with a chopper. Led out to execution on a tumbril, her body nipped thrice with red-hot tongs, then beheaded with the sword, standing; her head fixed on a pole above and her body buried under the gallows.

51. Two thieves hanged.

52. A thief hanged.

53. November 17th. Hans Müllner of Litzendorf (60 years old) *alias* der Schmeisser, who, while on a road with his sister, as they returned from their usual work, she being pregnant, slew and murdered her on the road with premeditation and dealt lustfully with her, then buried the body in a field. Executed on the wheel at Nuremberg.

54. December 6th. Anna Strölin of Grefenberg, a murderess, who with premeditation murdered and slew her own child, a boy of six years of age, with a chopper. She was minded to murder the other four children, but they moved her pity, so that she desisted. Beheaded with the sword at Nuremberg.

Total : 20 persons.

Year 1581

55. January 10th. Christoff Hauck, *alias* the Fiddling Cobbler, from Neuenstadt on the Aysch, a shoemaker by trade, also a fiddler and drummer and a great thief ; he also played the jester at the town festivals ; hanged at Nuremberg ; took leave of the world as a Christian. Had been spared the gallows 12 years before at Culmbach.

56. May 25th. Henssla Humbsen of Lambretzhoffen, *alias* Adam ; Merdta Herdegen of Schwabach, *alias* Henna and Stürer Merta ; George Hiss of Sultzbach, *alias* Hegelregler or Sultz-Kürchner ; three thieves and robbers, who attacked people by night in their houses and in lonely farms, bound them, tortured them and did violence to them, robbing them of money and clothes. All three hanged at Nuremberg.

57. June 1st. George Presigel of Gnotzga, who killed his wife and afterwards hanged her so that it might be supposed she had hanged and destroyed herself ; had also formerly stabbed a man. Beheaded with the sword at Nuremberg. Dissected, that is to say, cut up.

58. A horse-thief hanged.

59. August 10th. George Schörpff of Ermb, near the Hohenstein, a lecher, guilty of beastliness with four cows, two calves, and a sheep. Beheaded for unnatural vice at Velln, and afterwards burnt together with a cow.

60. A thief hanged ; had previously served in the galleys.

61. October 26th. Michael Passelt of Sultzbach, a pursemaker's hand, who was wedded both to his mistress, called Maglin, and her daughter, having long lived in lecherous intimacy with them. Beheaded with the sword here in Nuremberg ; his body afterwards burnt.

Total : 9 persons.

Year 1582

62. February 20th. Catherine Bücklin, a native of Bürckenstatt, formerly called ' Stamlet Kathra ' and ' the foreigner,' whom my father formerly whipped out of the town of Preseck with rods. Lately, consorting with thieves and robbers, formed a band of sixteen, attacked people by night at Mossfühl, at Esterfeld and at

the mill near Würzburg, also at Pühel and Hennau and many other places. Bound their victims, tortured, beat and wounded them, forced and extorted money from them, robbed and stole their clothes. Beheaded with the sword at Nuremberg. She should have been executed on the same day twelve weeks earlier, but obtained a respite on the pretext of pregnancy; which was not true.

63. A man beheaded for violating a girl of fourteen.

64. July 17th. Ursula Becherin of Hessdorf, an incendiary, who in the year 1580 burnt a stall belonging to her master, a farmer on the Marelstein, because the old people were harsh (to her), and in this year 1582 she did the same to her master, a farmer at Haselhoff, on the Friday before St. John's day, also stealing the clothes of the farmer and his man, and this only because she could do nothing right in their opinion. Beheaded in Nuremberg with the sword, standing, and afterwards burnt.

65. A man hanged for killing his wife, who was pregnant.

66. Anna Bischoffin of Augsburg, *alias* die

Feyhl, formerly whipped out of Würzburg and branded on the cheeks. Set fire to a shed at Kützen farm at Lauff on St. John Baptist's day on account of a purse, which she had mislaid and thought it had been stolen from her. Beheaded with the sword, standing, at Lauff, her body burnt, her head set up on the scaffold. Gave out she was pregnant, thinking to obtain a respite, but it was not true.

67. A woman, who murdered her own infant, beheaded.

68. A thief hanged.

Total : 7 persons.

Year 1583

69. A thief hanged.

70. A thief beheaded as a favour.

71. September 12th. George Götzn of Nuremberg, who had twice been whipped out of Nuremberg with rods and also sent to the galleys because of his thefts, but now, together with his companion, killed a carrier in a wood at Bruckthann, took his money and left the horse and cart. Hans Rotter of Schmiedtfelt,

a weaver and a thief. Both beheaded with the sword (and not hanged) as a favour, at Nuremberg.

72. November 26th. Hans Welcker, a thimble-maker of Nuremberg, *alias* der Mennla, who cheated in gaming and had been sent to the galleys on that account and whipped out of the town, and had suffered the same at Regensburg. Beheaded with the sword at Nuremberg.

73. A man beheaded for murdering another during a quarrel.

74. December 10th. Hans Popp, a blacksmith at Nuremberg, 22 years old, who entered many shops and warehouses with false keys he had manufactured for the purpose, and stole things from them—the keys were thrown upon the gallows—beheaded with the sword at Nuremberg.

Total : 7 persons.

Year 1584

75. A church-thief hanged. His father had also been hanged.

76. A thief hanged.

77. February 11th. Maria Kürschnerin of Nuremberg, *alias* Silly Mary, who had formerly been whipped out of the town with rods, and had her ears cropped; also Katherine Schwertzin of Weher, *alias* Country Kate, who had also formerly been whipped out of the town; both of them thieves and whores, who with thievish youths and fellows climbed and broke into citizens' houses and stole a mighty quantity of things; both hanged at Nuremberg. It was an unheard of thing for a woman to be hanged in Nuremberg, and it had never yet happened. (*See Part II., No. 63.*)

78. February 12th. Hennsa of Geyselwind, *alias* the fat lad; Hennsa Pallauf of Hernda; Killian Wurmb of Virnspach, *alias* Backendt; Hans Schober of Wcher, *alias* Pulfferla; and Hennssla Klopffer of Reigelsdorff; five thieves who, with the previously executed 'Silly Mary' and 'Country Kate,' had burgled and stolen (they had also formerly been whipped out and put in the stocks ten times). They had to be clothed, for they were naked and bare; some of them knew no prayers and had never been

in a church ; the eldest were 22, 17, 16 and 15 years old, the youngest 13 years. All five hanged here in Nuremberg.

79. A thief hanged.

80. March 24th. Heinrich Heut of Büch, *alias* the Shopman, a thief and murderer. Killed a carrier who had driven to the town for thirty years, and took his money, also took 60 florins from a carter of Grundla at Bruck ; took 17 florins from another carter in the little oakwood near Thennalohe, 6 florins from another carrier behind Schwabach, also stole 4 horses. Executed on the wheel at Nuremberg.

81. A murderer beheaded.

82. Anna Peyelstainin of Nuremberg, *alias* Moser Annala, because she had carnal intercourse with a father and a son, called ' die Doppengiesser ' (who themselves both had wives, she having a husband), and similarly with twenty-one married men and youths, her husband conniving ; was beheaded here with the sword, standing. Her husband, called Jerome Peyelstain, was whipped out of the town. He wrote these lines on the wall of St. Peter's Church, near her grave : ' Father and son

should have been treated as she was, and the panders also. In the other world I shall summon Emperor and King because justice has not been done. I, poor man, suffer though innocent. Farewell and good night.'

83. A robber beheaded.

84. A thief hanged.

85. Two church-thieves hanged.

86. October 16th. Peter Köchl, of Hirschbach near Hersspruch, a peasant, who beat his father for the third time—he beat him so badly, seven years ago, that he was condemned to the loss of his right hand at Schnatta, but bought the hand off with a hundred florins—this time however he again lay in wait for his father in the Schleegasse at Hersspruch and inflicted seven wounds on him, leaving him for dead. Beheaded at Nuremberg ; was dissected and cut up.

87. November 17th. Anna Freyin, a cloth-worker of Nuremberg. Having brought forth a child by a cutler called Ambrosius (she having formerly been married); the child being a boy, and two years old, she threw it in the well by the Franciscan Church and drowned it,

afterwards going to the prison voluntarily. Beheaded with the sword here.

Total : 20 persons.

Year 1585

88. February 11th. Frederick Werner of Nuremberg, *alias* Heffner Friedla, a murderer and a robber who committed three murders and twelve robberies. The first time he shot dead his own companion at Büch, the second time he killed and robbed a man in the Erlanger Wood, the third time he killed a journeyman, whom he attacked alone in the Fischbach Wood and knocked on the head with a stone, so that he died here in hospital. He likewise helped to rob his wife in the Schwabach Wood with the help of Herdtelt (already executed) and left her for dead. Drawn to execution in a tumbril, twice nipped with red-hot tongs, and afterwards broken on the wheel.

89. Three thieves hanged.

90. February 18th. Hans Meller of Gostenhoff, a tiler, *alias* Reuter Henssla, a thief and cheat at gaming, who also married three wives, hanged at Nuremberg. He said to the judges

in court, as he left it : " God guard you ; for dealing thus with me you will have to see a black devil one day," and as he was led out to execution he gave vent to all kinds of arrogance and sang two songs at the gallows : ' When my hour is at hand,' and ' Let what God wills always happen.' During the first night a pair of red knitted stockings was put on him as he hung on the gallows.

91. A murderer beheaded.

92. October 15th. Hanss Hoffmann of Obersdorff, a thief, who stole clothes from the sick in the Lazaret, and had broken the Ban six times. Because he was caught in the act at the Lazaret, an honourable council ordered the sentence to be read in front of the Lazaret by a town-beadle. He was then led out to the place of execution and hanged ; such a proceeding had never been heard of before.

93. Four burglars hanged.

Total : 11 persons.

Year 1586

94. A thief hanged.

95. Two thieves hanged.

96. A murderer beheaded.

97. A robber beheaded as a favour.

98. August 4th. Hans Weber, of the New Town, a potter and thief, whom I whipped out of Neunkirchen ten years ago ; Lienhardt Hagen, of Teüsslen, a bath-keeper, *alias* der Kaltbader, a thief and robber, who with his companion helped to attack people by night, tortured them, burnt them with fire, poured hot grease on them and wounded them grievously; also tortured pregnant women, so that one died at Schwertzenbach ; stole all manner of things everywhere. The potter was hanged, the bath-keeper executed on the wheel. The bath-keeper had broken into the church at Lohndorff and stolen the chalice, also helped once to steal 500 florins (*a list of many other small sums follows*).

99. A murderer beheaded.

100. November 22nd. Lienhardt Bardtmann of Aldorf, a horseman, Peter Knaup of Gaslenhoff, a tailor, both thieves and harbourers of thieves. Lienhardt, together with his companions, entered by stealth the dwelling of the robe-maker by the Fleischbrucken (bridge) when the master was absent and only two maids

in the house (a servant who had formerly served there giving information). They shut themselves up in the house during the night and stole 2,200 florins' worth of silver articles, chains, rings, bracelets. Knaup, the tailor, harboured this gang and helped to divide, weigh, pawn and sell such stolen goods, and himself stole also. Both the above-mentioned hanged at last as thieves at Nuremberg. Lienhardt's last words, as he stood on the ladder and was about to die, were that he had been called ' the horseman ' for a long time, but now he would really learn to ride ; he feared however he would remain hanging with his head in the stirrup. He remained hanging for only three days in the place of execution, then someone cut through his neck, so that the head alone remained hanging and the body fell to the ground. The cause was this. When some lewd fellows lay imprisoned near him, he informed them that he had much gold sewn in his clothes, and that if they cut him down when he was hanged they would get good booty. Nothing was found, however.

Total : 11 persons.

Year 1587

101. January 5th. Hans Krauss of Burcken-statt, *alias* Locksmith Hans, a burglar of churches, who broke into the church at Endt-mannsberg with his companions, stole the chalice and vestments and broke open four trunks, also attacked people in their houses by night. He was captured at Betzenstein, brought in and hanged at Nuremberg.

102. A thief hanged.

103. A horse-thief hanged.

104. A thief hanged.

105. June 8th. Lienhardt Günther of Lang-enzenn, *alias* Dattelweber, an incendiary, who ten years ago without any cause burnt down at Fach a barn full of corn valued at 500 florins, and a year ago burnt down the farm of a farmer of Eckersdorff, called Weiller, together with the corn, cattle, fodder and all other contents, doing damage to the extent of 2,000 florins, which farm cost 3,000 florins to rebuild. Besides, he sought to blackmail the farmer, threatening to burn down his farm again. On this account he was beheaded as a special favour and his body afterwards burnt. Was worthy of a worse fate.

106. July 20th. Gertrude Schmidtin of Fach, a peasant girl and heretic. She lived in debauchery for four years with her own father and brother, who were burnt alive at Langenzenn a week later. Beheaded with the sword as a favour.

107. Two highway robbers beheaded as a favour.

108. August 29th. Elizabeth Rossnerin of Leibsgrüen, a day-labourer and beggar, who smothered and throttled her companion, also a field-worker, and took 4 pounds 9 pfennigs from her. Beheaded with the sword as a favour, because she was a poor creature and had a wry neck.

109. October 3rd. Margaret Brechtlin, daughter of the tax-collector at the Spittlerthor, who gave her husband Hans Prechteln (a carpenter in Gastenhof) insect-powder in porridge, also in eggs, although he did not die at once of it. Beheaded with the sword and not hanged, as a favour.

110. October 17th. Christopher Schmiedt of Nuremberg, *alias* Cooper Chris, a cooper and thief, who was banished the land for his thefts.

Lately entered eight rooms at the public baths, wearing old clothes, and when he went out put on the better ones of other people, leaving his old ones in their place ; also stole many things in other places.   Hanged here.

111. A murderer and robber executed on the wheel.

Total : 12 persons.

Year 1588

112. January 2nd. George Hörnlein of Bruck, Jobst Knau of Bamberg, a potter, both of them murderers and robbers.   Two years ago Hörnlein and a companion attacked a carrier on the Remareuth, stabbed him four times so that he died, and took 32 florins. Six weeks ago he and Knau were consorting with a whore. She bore a male child in the house, where Knau baptised it, then cut off its hand while alive.   Then a companion, called Schwarz, tossed the child in the air, so that it fell upon the table, and said : " Hark how the devil whines ! " then cut its throat and buried it in the little garden belonging to the house.

A week later the above-mentioned Hörnlein and Knau, when the whore of the aforesaid Schwarz bore a child, wrung its neck; then Hörnlein, cutting off its right hand, buried it in the yard of the house. Six weeks ago Hörnlein and Knau with a companion, a certain Weisskopf, attacked a man between Herzog and Frauen Aurach. Knau shot him dead, took 13 florins, dragged the body into the wood and covered it with brushwood. (*A long list of murders and highway robberies follows here. Schmidt adds*) : To conclude it would require another half sheet to write down all the people they attacked (*further details added*). The two murderers were led out on a tumbril. Both their arms were twice nipped with red-hot tongs, and their right arms and legs broken ; lastly they were executed on the wheel.

113. January 11th. George Mayer of Gostenhoff, *alias* Weisskopff, who with the abovementioned Hörnlein and Knauen robbed and murdered people, also Hainz Baum previously mentioned. and Utz Koler of Memmingen, formerly twice whipped out of our town, all

executed ; Mayer, as a murderer, on the wheel, Baum and Koler with the rope. Weisskopff often pleaded epilepsy ; when he was about to be examined by torture he fell into a fit and pretended the illness tormented him. As he had been excused three days before on this pretext, he taught his companions to do likewise, so that they would be let off ; but when Knau also tried to do this he was not successful.

114. Margaret Hörnlein of Bruck, who harboured her husband together with Knau and Weisskopff, the above-mentioned robbers and thieves; was also accessory to the murder of the newly-born children who were killed in her house, and gave all the men food so that they might not inform about anything—put to death by drowning.

115. A thief hanged.

116. May 28th. Hans Ramsperger, a wiredrawer and ex-citizen of this town ; thrice broke the Ban ; was employed as a betrayer and informer by the Margraviate. He betrayed many citizens of Nuremberg and other states, of whom nine or ten were executed, and many

who pleaded innocence suffered mangling of the limbs and torture, when nothing was found against them. He also betrayed the town of Nuremberg, revealing where the walls were weakest and most easily stormed and offering to do his best to bring this to pass, also to betray Master Weyermann or bring him to prison. For these reasons he was captured at Eldersdorf and beheaded here as a favour, his body quartered, the four limbs being fixed at the corners (of the scaffold) and the head on a pole above.

As was recorded eighty-four years ago, in the year 1504, in the times of the Margrave Casimir, an informer (in the pay) of the Margrave was executed here in the same way; which man, when he lay captive in prison for his crime, being put in the Water-Tower[1] here, and permitted to work at wire-drawing to pay his debts, made a ladder of this wire, descended from the tower, and betook himself at once to his treason again. He was caught again, but exculpated himself and was released. Later he was arrested and imprisoned, and thereafter had to sign a pledge and oath in the court

[1] See the illustration facing p. 75 (*Wasser-thurm*).

record-book, never to quit the town; this promise he did not keep, however, but once more took to his treason.

117. July 4th. Hans Völckla of Onoltzbach, *alias* Hemmerlein, a chief-ranger of the Margrave, was arrested at Rötenbach on June 16th for having been a declared enemy of the Nurembergers; he had been so bold as to seize the snares of the fowlers, which he was not authorised to do; also took their wares from the pedlars. Two years ago he had a dispute with Hans Monich, a sugar-worker, and they shot at each other; then he, Hemmerlein, cried to his (assistant) game-keeper to shoot the sugar-worker, and the former sent a bullet and some shot through the sugar-worker's body, but he did not die of it.

In the year 1587 Hemmerlein with many others (*a list of names and other details follows*) shot three men. He was beheaded with the sword as a favour. It was on that occasion that some cannon were placed on the walls, some sharpshooters posted, and precautions taken against an attack by the Margrave's men. Orders were also given to me, Master Franz the executioner, at the bidding of an honourable councillor, Master Hans Nützel, that I should put him to death on the bridge or elsewhere in case the Margrave's men attacked us, so that they might not find him alive. All passed off quietly, then he was taken to a tower on Wednesday, in the presence of a Syndic of the Margrave, and at night he was taken to the town-prison. A reprieve was refused and he was executed early in the morning.

118. September 3rd. George Solen of Nuremberg, a blanket-weaver, *alias* Leck-Küchner, brought up in the Foundling Hospital, a thief who broke into houses and gardens many times and stole from them ; was whipped out of the town three months ago. Hanged here and left on the gallows only eight days, for someone cut down half his body with the breeches and left the rest hanging. The body was finally thrown into the gallows pit next day, as it looked too horrible.

119. Three thieves hanged.

Total : 13 persons.

Year 1589

120. A thief hanged.

121. do.

122. do.

123. Franz Seuboldt of Strölnfels, citizen of Grefenberg, who lay in wait for his own father (a steward at Osternohe) upon his fowling-ground. He hid behind a rock, covering himself with brushwood, and when his father climbed a pole (which they call Anpfahl) to take down the decoy-bird, shot him with a charge of four bullets, so that he died next day. Although no one knew who had done it, as he fled from the place he dropped and lost a glove while running, which glove a tailor at Grefenberg had patched for him the day before, and this was found by a woman, thus revealing the deed. The year before he had tried to poison him twice, but had not succeeded. For this crime he was led out in a tumbril, his body was nipped thrice with the red-hot tongs, then two of his limbs shattered with the wheel, and he was finally executed on it. Was brought over here from Grefenberg.

124. November 18th. Gabriel Heroldt, a

tailor and citizen and warden of the Frog Tower
here at Nuremberg (a man of advanced age),
because he forced Catherine Reichlin, who was
under his charge as a prisoner, to commit
debauchery; and the year previously tried to
do the same with a girl of thirteen who boarded
at his house, he being her guardian, but did not
succeed because of her youth—was beheaded
here with the sword as a favour, and not hanged.

Total: 5 persons.

Year 1590

125. March 24th. Hans Walter of Betzenstein, *alias* Keesheckel, who was brought here
from Hilpertstein ; a thief who took part in the
attack on the mill at Pernthal (where the miller
was robbed of about 500 florins) with the help
of fourteen companions and two whores, also
stole many things elsewhere—hanged in this
town.

126. April 2nd. George Schweiger of Falck-
endorf near Herzogaurach, a thief who, in his
youth, together with his brother, first stole
40 florins from his own father. Later, when his

father sent him to settle a debt, he kept the money and gambled with it ; lastly, discovering that his father had a treasure buried in a barn behind the house, he stole 60 florins of it. He had a lawful wife, but left her and attached himself to two whores, promising marriage to both. Beheaded with the sword as a favour. His father let him lie in prison here, and desired and insisted that justice should be done, in spite of the fact that he had recovered his money.

127. A woman who murdered her infant beheaded.

128. A thief hanged.

129. A church-thief hanged.

130. July 7th. Margaret Schwamberger of Arletzhofen, a peasant-girl, who having borne a child by Contz Kerlin of Great Mainfallen, murderously stabbed it with a knife in the left breast ; she also cut its throat and cast its body into a manure pit. She was arrested at Mainfallen and beheaded at Felden. Her head was fixed to the gallows.

131. July 28th. Frederick Stigler of Nuremberg, a smith and executioner's assistant, for

having brought accusations against some burghers' wives, for that, he said, they were witches and he knew it by certain signs—however, he wittingly did them wrong—also that they dealt in witchcraft and spells ; likewise for having threatened his brother Peter, on account of which threat he had appeared before the court at Bamberg, but was begged off ; lastly, for having taken a second wife during the life of his first wife, and a third wife during the life of the second, after the death of the first—was beheaded with the sword here as a favour instead of being hanged.

132. A thief beheaded.

133. Two thieves hanged.

134. September 24th. Moses the Jew, of Otenfoss, residing at Ermreuth, a thief and Nuremberg spy, who broke into Heroldt's inn at Rückersdorff three or four times (*here follows a long list of petty thefts from carriers and servants at inns*), and also stole anything he could snap up among Jews—strangled here, as a special favour, in front of the law court. It is 54 years since a Jew was executed. This Jew was

arrested at the above-mentioned Heroldt's inn and brought here.

135. Two thieves hanged.

136. December 8th. Hans Gering of Stockig, a peasant and thief who, at Closter Neuburg on the Thona, two miles above Vienna, stole two horses from a miller he had served, sold one for 23 florins and the other for 18 florins at Gostenhoff; also stole many other things—beheaded here on his own petition, and then dissected, that is, cut up. Was brought in here from Greffenburg.

Total : 14 persons.

Year 1591

137. A thief hanged.

138. A murderer beheaded.

139. May 18th. Hans Fröschel, a woodturner and citizen of Nuremberg, a thief, who introduced himself everywhere into houses with his work, when he executed orders, and stole cloaks, namely one at Von Thil's house (*here other houses are mentioned*), also snatched mantles from maids at night in the streets—arrested at

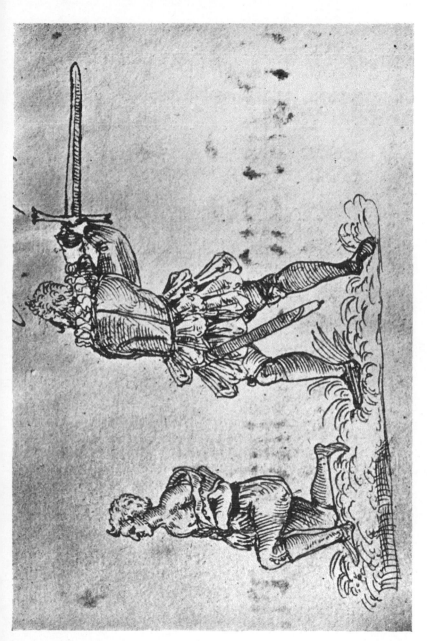

THE EXECUTION OF HANS FRÖSCHEL BY MASTER FRANZ SCHMIDT

MAY 18TH, 1591. (SEE DIARY, NO. 139)

A CONTEMPORARY PEN-AND-INK SKETCH, STATE ARCHIVES OF NUREMBERG

(face p. 144)

Lauff, brought in here and beheaded with the sword by his own request.

140. May 25th. Conrad Prückner, of Schwernitz above Lichtenfels (a serious man), who had been town-beadle at Schesslitz for 9 years and 8 years at Bamberg, a murderer, who shot the young servant of an Italian trader in a wood near Bechoffen and took from him some spices in two boxes and three lengths of fustian, afterwards leaving the body on the spot—beheaded with the sword here as a favour, and exposed on the wheel.

141. Matthew Lenger of Eulenburg, a cooper and citizen of this town, also a traitor and thief, who forced his way into the house of the woman Ortel in the New Buildings, broke open chests in the parlour and bedrooms, stealing many clothes, pewter-ware and five candlesticks; Wolf Lenckher, son of a citizen here, called 'the big Nuremberger,' a thief who stole many articles at Frankfort fair; broke into many shops at Nuremberg with his companion, taking the money from them—both men hanged. The cooper was stripped naked the first night, except for his stockings, so

that a shirt and trunk-hose had to be put on him.

Total: 6 persons.

Year 1592

142. A thief hanged.

143. do.

144. April 11th. Stoffel Weber, a plasterer and member of St. Mark's brotherhood, because he with Peckschlager Erla and a wire-drawer snatched their weapons from Hans Heer and his servant by night, pointed them at their breasts and tried to steal their cloaks. Should have been beheaded, but he was begged off and his life was granted him. In the year 1588 Hemmerlein's servant (*see No.* 117) who shot Monig the sugar-worker (he did not die, however) was also reprieved ; previously also the man Rosentaler, who had carried on a tricky smuggling trade at Verona in Italy with the help of the bandits, was similarly reprieved ; formerly also a peasant of Herspruck who, after drinking with another in an inn, rose from his drink and went in to the peasant's wife by night, as if he

were her husband, then got up and left her, but was recognised as a stranger by the woman when she looked after him—was also reprieved. In the year 1576 a tradesman, who had become the father of a child by his step-daughter, was also reprieved.

Total : 2 persons.

Year 1593

145. A thief hanged.

146. February 23rd. Lienhardt Kiesswetter of Upper Röhrnstatt, *alias* Linhardt Lubing, Linhardt of Röhrnstatt, Mosel Lindl and der Sichen Lindl, a robber and murderer, who attacked the inn-keeper on the Schlicht and struck him on the head so that he died ; helped in the burglary at Greding where Kohler's wife died ; likewise stabbed 'Black Nick' his companion ; helped to plunder a mill at Weissenburg (*a list of other robberies follows*) ; had 29 companions. Executed on the wheel at Sultzbach.

147. Two thieves hanged.

148. Stephen Rebweller of Maschstall, a

tradesman and thief who employed young thieves to cut purses, giving them a dollar a week apiece and their food; Henry Hausmann of Kalckha, 14 miles below Köln, George Müllner of Dornitz, a tradesman, *alias* Lean George, thieves, robbers, and murderers. Henry and Lean George took part in the burglary at Niederndorf, in which the Jew was killed. When Henry shot him, Lean George knocked him on the head so that he fell over a bench and remained lying there; then they carried away everything. In the same way Henry with the aid of companions committed four more burglaries, but Lean George with his companions murdered at Summersfeld a shopkeeper called Schedl, who had also been their companion, and took his property; likewise next day he murdered the same Schedl's wife in a little wood between Rohr and Allersberg, suffocating her with a kerchief she had round her neck, then robbed her of her money and clothes. (*A list of other robberies with violence committed by George follows here.*) He took part besides in committing other burglaries and thefts. For these crimes Stephen Rebweller was first hanged as a

thief ; the other two murderers, Henry Haussmann and Lean George, being executed on
the wheel. George had two limbs shattered
first.

(*A long list of the names of George Müllner's
confederates in crime follows here, then a list of
Henry Haussmann's companions.*)

149. A thief hanged and a highway robber
beheaded.

150. July 3rd. Bartholomew Matzeroth of
Milan, a chimney sweep and thief, who borrowed
4 royal dollars of David Kresser under a false
name and took two pair of embroidered silk
stockings from his cousins at Chur in Switzerland, ten crowns and two gold bracelets here at
Murmann's house, a piece of velvet from his
cousins at Costnitz, was beheaded with the
sword as a special favour; he had been in prison
at Anspach and had broken out ; as he was a
catholic he received the sacrament ; when he was
being led out and the bell had tolled, he was
granted the favour (of being beheaded) as he
should have been hanged.

151. July 10th. Conrad von Reichensachsen,
from Hesse, a baptized Jew, whose sponsors

were Julius Echter, bishop of Würzburg, and Count Conrad of Schwarzburg, a murderer and thief who knocked on the head with a birchwood cudgel the son of one of our citizens in a little wood near Höchstadt, as he was on his way to the Netherlands. After that he struck him with the weapon and stabbed him with a knife nine times, stripped him of his clothes and 3 florins he found on him, then left him lying there in his shirt (he died three days later) ; also stole many things at different times. Had been whipped out of the town with his gang on the 10th of July, 1592. Executed on the wheel, two of his limbs being broken first ; would not receive the (? Lutheran) sacrament, but desired it in the catholic way.

152. October 11th. Gabriel Wolff, of a burgher's family here, who called himself George Windholz, Secretary to the Elector at Berlin, also took the name of Ernst Haller and Joachim Fürnberger, borrowed 1,500 ducats from a councillor here in Nuremberg by means of a forged letter in the Elector's name and under the seal of the Margrave John George in Berlin; was arrested at Regensburg and delivered over

to Nuremberg. Besides this he practised many such forgeries; for instance he demanded 2,000 dollars of a councillor at Danzig in the King of Sweden's name, but when the fraud was discovered received nothing. (*A list of similar frauds and forgeries follows.*) He absconded with 1,400 crowns in the Netherlands and travelled to Turkey. When in Constantinople, on the death of Jacob Führer, he took the latter's signet ring, books, and clothes, with a few dollars; the clothes were taken from him at sea, but he kept the ring. In Italy he tried to abduct an abbess, but failed; he took, however, a silver gilt striking clock from her sister. On another occasion he took a silver clock from a Knight of St. John called Master George, as well as a horse, and rode away. In Prague, where he was the Emperor's personal attendant, being charged with pawning a lady's silver goblets and girdle for 12 florins, he stole (them) and sold them for 40 florins; also practised many other frauds, causing false seals of gentlemen to be cut, wrote many forged documents and was conversant with seven years. Beheaded with the sword here at Nuremberg, the body being afterwards burnt. Should have had his right hand cut off first, this being decided and ordered, but was subsequently spared this.

153. A thief beheaded, his body dissected.

Total : 13 persons.

Year 1594

154. A thief, who stole bee-hives and other articles, hanged.

155. Two thieves hanged.

156. July 23rd. Hans Schatz, a wire-drawer, who for four years stole wire from Trammel and from Kandler, both wire-drawers, and buried it; he sold 45 florins' worth of Trammel's property and 13 florins of Kandler's; of the rest of the wire several hundredweights were dug up. Beheaded with the sword as a favour.

157. A thief hanged.

158. August 13th. Christopher Mayer, a weaver of fustian, and Hans Weber, a fruiterer, both citizens of this town, who for three years

had practised sodomy together and were informed against by a hook-maker's apprentice,
who caught them in the act behind a hedge.
The fruiterer had practised this for twenty years,
that is with the cook Endressen, with Alexander,
and others. The weaver was first beheaded,
then his body was burnt with the fruiterer,
who was burnt alive.

159. Two young thieves, aged 16, beheaded.

Total : 9 persons.

Year 1595

160. January 2nd. Fritz Wolffel of Greffenberg, a robber, who, accompanied by his brother,
but acting alone, knocked down with a cudgel
and caused to fall under his horse a peasant of
Katzwann and took 14 florins from him. Beheaded here with the sword for this, and exposed
on the wheel.

161. January 23rd. George Haffner of Michel-
feld, a scrivener, who served in the house of
the Burgrave of Rottenberg and stole many
things there ; was whipped out of Sulzbach
for this ; after that he copied the seals of the

Burgrave's wife and of Simon Hecktor by engraving on lead with a shoemaker's awl. Afterwards he wrote forged letters and obtained 40 florins at Hetzold's house and other places. Beheaded with the sword here as a favour instead of being hanged.

162. March 29th. George Franck of Poppenreuth, a smith's man and *Lanzknecht*,[1] who persuaded Fair Anna to let him escort her to meet Martin Schönherlin her betrothed at Pruck on the Leuth; and when he, with Christopher Frischen, also a *Lanzknecht*, had brought her into a wood, the two having made a plot about her, Christopher struck her on the head with a stake from behind, so that she fell; then dealt two more blows as she lay there. Franck also struck her once or twice and then cut her throat. They stripped her of everything except her shift, and left her there and sold the clothes at Durn Hembach for 5 florins; all this happening on St. Andrew's day in the year '93. Besides, he made false seals and he forged documents, thinking to obtain money by them, but did not succeed. Also he was

---

[1] A mercenary soldier, who fought as a pikeman.

imprisoned for a year and a half in Vienna, because of two horses he stole from his master with the help of a stable-boy. For these crimes he was broken on the wheel here, being condemned to a stroke on each arm and a third on the chest.

163. July 19th. Ulrich Lösser of Eschenbach, a peasant living at Herspruck, who set fire at night to his neighbour Brunner's house, but when the house was saved, so that only one side was burnt down by daybreak, he helped to put the fire out; then threw burning straw on the shed, intending to set it alight. Suspected for this reason, he was punished for the fire; and because of this he withdrew, threatening to burn down the village if they did not give him 50 or 60 florins to make up for his punishment. Beheaded as a favour at Herspruck, his body afterwards burnt.

164. September 10th. Hans Weckler of Möhrnstadt near Würzburg, a tailor and thief, who stole 200 florins by night from a tailor at Gold Cronach, taking them out of a wallet and substituting sand; but he gambled away the money, which he was cheated of by

Gronla and Rosala (he sued them for it and they were whipped out of the city). He also stole 25 florins from an innkeeper and besides took 5 florins from three women. Hanged here.

165. November 6th. Hans Sigert of Pollingen near Neuenmark, a farm hand who murdered a tailor named Summerlein, at Sünderspühl, with a triangular fence post. Beheaded here ; wept all the way until he knelt down.

166. A thief beheaded as a favour.

Total : 7 persons.

Year 1596

167. A thief hanged.

168. Two coiners beheaded and the body of one afterwards burnt. (*A note states that Franz bungled the execution.*)

169. A thief beheaded as a favour.

170. March 11th. Hans Wolff Marti, citizen of Wehr, a tradesman who committed sodomy in many places at various times, first with a bargeman at Ibss, with another at Brauningen, with a peasant at Miltenburck (*a list of other*

SECTION OF A PLAN OF NUREMBERG IN 1596

FROM A DRAWING ON WOOD BY PAUL PFINZING VON HENFENFELD, IN STATE ARCHIVES OF NUREMBERG

(face p. 156)

persons follows)—beheaded with the sword as a favour ; his body afterwards burnt.

171. June 4th. George Praun, of Windisch, *alias* Pihn Georg, who was at feud with a peasant and lay in wait for him ; also stole many things with the help of his brother ' Pihnhaintz,' who was executed here. As a favour and by his request he was beheaded here. Had a neck two spans long and two hands' breadth thick.

172. June 6th. Sebald Humpelmann of Offenhausen, a poacher who had previously been banished from the land, but again shot game and shot the groom of the bailiff at Roth ; beheaded with the sword as a favour instead of being hanged.

173. July 22nd. Hans Niclaus of Koburg, *alias* The Scholar ; Hans Schmidt of Zerrndorf, *alias* Geybert or Henssa von Zerrndorf ; both thieves and brothers-in-law. Schmidt was also a murderer, who with other companions committed three burglaries ; the first at the forester's house at Rotenberg, whom he robbed of everything ; the second at Mühlgrund near Hochstedt at the inn kept by a woman, whom he wounded ; the third at Hetzeldorf near

Ebermanstadt, in a house where two families lived, wounding the people so cruelly that one woman received 17 wounds, blows, or stabs, of which she died after 13 weeks; the other had her hand hacked off and died three days after. For these crimes Niclaus was executed with the rope, as a thief, and Schmidt on the wheel, as a murderer.

174. December 2nd. Hans Krauss of Kemmethen near Neunmark, and Christopher Hoffmann of Nuremberg, both thieves; Krauss, who had been imprisoned here five times, broke into houses here and stole much, being caught at last at Schmiedburger's house; Hoffmann and his companion climbed into houses by means of ladders at night and stole many things. Also, when he was out five weeks ago in the meadows belonging to the Teutschen Herren with his companion who helped him in burglaries, he fixed a flint in his gun and, wishing to try it, fired the gun; but not noticing his companion, shot him dead (although unintentionally). Then he pushed the body into the water near the willows and left it there. Both hanged here for these crimes.

Total: 11 persons.

Year 1597

175. February 10th. Anna Feygneri (called von Greffenberg after her father and Eyssmeyin after her husband), a thief who was whipped out of Nuremberg on July 30th, 1595; twice married, both husbands executed. Also Dietrich Mayr of Dittnhofen, known as George and also as the Black Monk and the Buffoon, who had been her paramour; and Peter Rainstecken of Osternoh, *alias* 'laudemus,' an emissary and spy of the Margraviate, both thieves. The woman Feygneri was beheaded, sitting on a stool; Mayr and Rainstecken hanged.

176. Two thieves hanged.

177. March 11th. Hans Frauhammer of Schwatz in Switzerland, called himself Andrew, also known as ' the foreigner ' and Hennssa ; and Wisner of Moss, *alias* the ' lad from Tella ' ; two thieves, who stole much at various times ; hanged at Sultzbach. Frauenhammer behaved wildly and gave trouble.

178. March 15th. Hans Haylandt of Statt Hilboldstein, a barber-surgeon, residing at Marck-Hamarck on the Main in Franconia, and Veronica Köllin of Gold Kranach, a

peasant girl, both executed—Haylandt because he and his companion Killian Ayrer went out with a young man who had been servant to a gentleman at Frankfort, and at midnight, when they stopped to drink at the fountain at Aschenburg, knocked him on the head, Haylandt then cutting his throat and robbing him of 200 florins; which money they knew he carried, and had asked the lad's master if they could take him with them. They had planned this murderous attack at Frankfort and, when they had carried it out, they tied a stone to the lad's girdle and threw him into the Main there. The deed was revealed next day when the dogs scratched up the blood, which had been covered over, and the owner of the vineyard at Aschenburg looked for the stone they had wrenched out of the wall and found the body in the water. After the two had divided the money between them, the barber-surgeon travelled to Nuremberg, and the father of the murdered lad followed him and had him arrested here. The woman Köllin, having given birth in her brother's house to a child by a farm-labourer, and as the babe, a girl, squealed a little, she, supposing her brother's wife who was in the kitchen might hear it, held its mouth with two fingers and suffocated it. When she buried it early in the morning, a washerwoman saw her and the deed came to light. Both beheaded as a favour. Haylandt's body exposed on the wheel and Köllin's head fixed on the gallows.

179. A thief and cutpurse, 16 years old, hanged.

180. August 16th. Carl Reichardt, called Eckerlein at Nuremberg, who was a simpleton; formerly whipped out of the town because of Schinbein's wife, with whom he had had immoral relations, as well as with other married women, stole here and everywhere from the executioners and their assistants, also at the knacker's yards where he lodged—beheaded with the sword here as a favour.

181. October 25th. Lorentz Schober of Mienitz, a thief who stole trifles, namely 12 loaves, 6 cheeses, a shirt and a doublet. At last he broke into the house of a poor woman at Gründlein, and when she caught him in the act and held him and screamed for help, he drew a knife and stabbed her thrice, the first time in the

head, the second time in the left breast, the third in the neck, and left her lying for dead, so that she recovered with difficulty. Beheaded for this with the sword as a favour and not hanged.

Total : 12 persons.

Year 1598

182. February 9th.   Elizabeth Aurholtin of Vielseck, who called herself ' die Gründlerin,' who tried to defraud people, giving out that she could conjure and dig up treasure, as she did with devilish incantations and ceremonies at the houses of Gipunckel, of a soldier's wife, of Counsellor Fischer's wife, etc.   This was how she carried out her tricks.   When she came into a house and wanted to cheat someone, she used to fall down as if she were ill or in convulsions, giving out afterwards that she had a wise vein hidden in her leg, whereby she could foretell and reveal future events and discover hidden treasures, and that when she entered a house her veins never left her in peace until she announced these things; also that the realms of earth were

opened out before her, and that she saw therein gold and silver, as if looking into a fire. If any doubted, she asked leave to spend the night in the house, so that she could speak with the spirit of the treasure. When this happened, she behaved at night, with her whisperings, questions, and answers, as if someone were speaking to her, and gave out afterwards that it was a poor lost soul that could not enter into bliss and that they must dig for treasure. Then the people let themselves be persuaded by her, believing such tales because of the horrible incantations which she used, and caused the ground to be dug up. During this digging she would slip a pot full of coals into the hole and give out that she had dug it up herself. This she commanded them to lock up in a chest for three weeks and not touch it, and then it would turn to gold. Meanwhile she decamped, and the coals remained coals. If some people did not believe her, she gave out she had drawn a fountain of gold for Master Endtress out of his yard and had dug up a golden treasure, nothing less than idols of pure gold. Master Baumgartner and Master Finoldt were guardians of her child. She had

4,000 florins in the treasury here. Beheaded here on account of her frauds. Had only one leg, and had to be carried out to execution.

183. March 30th. Christopher Neyner of Bodenstein, formerly residing at Leimburg, a horse-dealer who with a companion bought a horse of a peasant for 32 florins, which horse was to be paid for at Hirschau. As they were walking there with the peasant, he rode away on the horse and was caught with it at Eschenau. On other occasions he bought five horses and rode away with them; likewise rode away on his cousin's horse which was at pasture. Hanged for these deeds at Eschenau. No one had been hanged there for 76 years. (*See Part II., No. 232.*)

184. A murderer beheaded.

185. July 11th. Hans Kolben of Aylsdorf, a brickmaker, *alias* ' the long brickmaker ' and Brother Standfast, who stabbed his wife at Büch two years ago; also stabbed one of his companions on a road in Franconia. For this last crime he was imprisoned in a tower at Königshoffen, but loosening the stones with a bone he escaped. Likewise committed many deeds of

violence, attacking people at night. With a companion he forced, wounded, tortured and robbed these people at will; among them a peasant who tried to defend himself; whereupon he hacked him with an axe so that he died three days after. Likewise he coined many counterfeit dollars, three-kreutzer pieces and half-batzen pieces, which he sold at 25 dollars a hundred, and gave 200 pieces to the dicemaker (since executed) to dispose of, and could not tell himself how many he had made. Supposed he had coined many more than 2,000 pieces, apart from the three-kreutzer and half-batzen pieces. For this he was imprisoned in a tower at Klein Amburg, where he freed himself, took a rope and let himself down, but fell badly and bled severely, so that he had to lie in a wood for a whole day. He had also been in prison at Neuburg for coining and robberies, and there he broke a tile from a stove, took out a firebrand and held it to the bench till it burnt, and so freed himself from his chains and escaped. Because he could not escape from prison here he bit his left arm, cutting through the veins. When he was healed of this and led out on the last day, he bit out a piece of his right arm as large as a batzen piece and an inch deep, thinking he would thus bleed to death. For these crimes, as a murderer, robber, highwayman, and thief, who stole much many times, he had his four limbs broken on the wheel and was afterwards executed on it, and lastly his body was burnt. He pretended he could not walk, so that he had to be carried; did not pray at all, and bade the priest be silent, saying he knew it all beforehand and did not want to hear it, and that it made his head ache. God knows how he died.

186. August 3rd. Andrew Stayber of Crafft-shoff, a thief and tradesman who fifteen years ago stole a basin and 40 florins at Annersdorf, and two silver goblets and 8 florins from an inn-keeper at Birzl. From a Jew at Fürth he and four companions stole some bowls full of money, his share being 20 florins. Later, eight years ago, he and his companion Hans Dapffer (executed at Allerspach) stole from the same Jew 150 florins' worth of silver jewellery, and he sold his share to his companion for 10 florins. Also committed burglaries here frequently, and was expelled. Stole a quantity of fustian and linen

from a boat at Bamberg, selling his share for 12 florins. Stole many things besides in many places, but had given these practices up for five years and wanted to reform. Hanged here, as Kolb, who was executed (*p.* 164), gave evidence of his having been a thief.

187. November 14th. Hans Merckehl of Hamburg, *alias* Hirschen Hans, a farm-labourer and servant ; Hans Pörstner of Leuthenbach, *alias* Schmeltzlein, a peasant and horse-dealer ; both thieves. Schmeltzlein stole about 20 horses, selling them at different times. Merckehl, who was in service for 22 years, used to serve from half a year to two years in one place and when he left take away with him hose, doublets, boots, woollen shirts, and more in the way of money. When he drove some sheep to Augsburg for his master and obtained 35 florins for them, he ran away with the money. He did the same to his master at Amburg, who sent him with a horse and cart to fetch some white beer at Böhäm, running away with the horse and the money. He also stole a pair of hose and a doublet, in the pockets of which were 15 florins, which the thief was unaware of. Those who

pursued him caught him here. For these crimes the two thieves were hanged in this town. Pörstner said to the assistant hangman : " There's a pair of shoes for you and 5 florins besides, if you will exchange with me." These were his last words.

188. December 12th. Hans Ammon, from the castle at Forchhaim, a tailor, *alias* Waltznschneider, a thief who at Hopffnlohe, with a companion and his daughter, broke into the church and stole many vestments, also stole many things from other places; likewise rifled some bee-hives, and taught his daughter to steal; also filed false keys for burglary—was hanged here.

Total : 8 persons.

Year 1599

189. May 10th. Lienhardt Schwartz of Paydersholz near Roth, and Fritz Eysmann of Russelbach, *alias* Schlack, two thieves who stole many things at various times. Both beheaded with the sword as a favour. Schwartz, who had a knife about him, stabbed himself

twice in the stomach and then threw himself on the knife, but it did not pierce him ; also tore his shirt and tried to strangle himself with it, but did not succeed. Said a voice spoke to him, though he saw nobody, telling him that if he surrendered to him he would soon help him. At this he fell into repentance, but if the voice had called again it might have happened differently. He confessed the above when they were about to lead him out to death.

190. Two thieves beheaded as a favour.

191. August 7th. Peter Planck, a burgher of this town and a maker of cases, who after drinking heavily walked through the Spitler Gate towards the Schweinsteln on the evening of St. Peter and St. Paul's day, and saw a woman, who was a whore, walking in front of him along Sünderspelür Street and hurried after her. According to his account, she addressed him, asking him to go home with her, and when he refused she answered by a profanity or something of the kind. Then, as he sat down, she took away his hat, apparently to make a fool of him ; and he trying to recover it, they struggled together and he gave her a

blow in the face. Then she drew two knives and stabbed at him. Being thus attacked, he picked up some sand and threw it at her ; she did likewise, but when she pressed on him trying to stab him, he also drew out his knife and stabbed at her, wounding her eye, so that she fell and his knife broke in the act, leaving the haft in his hand. He knelt on her and snatched the knives from her hands, but his hand was cut by the blade and, being enraged, he drove the knife through her left breast as she lay there, so that it came out on her right side. For this he was beheaded here.

192. August 28th. Cuntz Stainla of Engelthal, a farm-hand, being in company with the son of the shepherd of Burcktan in the Bemmer Wood, three years ago, attacked three apprentices whom he met, at a quarter of a mile's distance from Stab. Although the two were unarmed except for pistols and the apprentices were armed, he shot one through the head, and the other two ran away. Then he stripped him of his mantle, which was blue with green-checked facings and edged with black braid. This he sold to a butcher at Stab, with whom

he had been half a year, for 1½ florins ; his companion however took a purse containing 12 florins out of the dead man's hose. Then they left the body and the bundle lying by the roadside. When an enquiry was made at Stab nothing was discovered, but he took service with the butcher. Because he did not deny it (afterwards) and also committed other small thefts, he was beheaded as a favour at Nuremberg. For if he had concealed it he would have escaped, as he betrayed himself when he said to the farm lad with whom he was playing marbles that if he had the courage to shoot a man in the Böhmer Wood, he would also have spirit enough to stake a ten-kreutzer piece. In this way his crime was discovered.

193. December 4th. Six Gom of Mitlschenbach, a vagabond and thief, *alias* Blind Sixt or Knollfinck, who with his wench and other thieves stole many things at different times, was beheaded here as a favour. Lay 23 weeks in prison ; was saved from the rope at the request of the Papists.

Total : 7 persons.

Year 1600

194. January 22nd. Veyt Willet of Günters-
bühl, a horse-dealer who swindled people over
purchases. Whenever he made a purchase it
was on deferred payment under a false name ;
he then rode away with the horse and was not
disposed to pay for it. Beheaded with the
sword here as a favour. He had previously
been whipped out of Pappenheim, likewise
out of Schwabach, where his ears were also
clipped. (*See Part II., No.* 224.)

195. A thief beheaded as a favour.

196. February 12th. George Mötzela, a
smith's son of Höchstatt, *alias* der Dolp, a
thief, the companion of Six Zans, who stole
much at various times, together with his wench
' fat Maygel ' (executed at Dachsbach three
days before him). Was in prison for three
quarters of a year because his boy, aged nine
years, the brother of his wench, accused him
of five murders, namely, of a pregnant woman
in Sebald's wood, of a man on Bundlach Hill,
of another at Heroldsberger's Well, and of one
at Thenalohe ; but there was no truth in all
this. Beheaded with the sword as a favour.

197. April 29th. Lienhardt Gösswein from near Weisenburg, and Lorentz Hirssperger of Burckstal, two thieves. Gösswein, who was caught in the cellar of the innkeeper Bastla's house at the Fruit Market intending to steal, had previously broken the grating of the cellar-trap at Pollet's house. He let himself down by means of a rope, broke open a desk, and stole 18 florins from it. Afterwards had come again but had not been able to enter. Was in possession of many tools.

Hirssperger had often been imprisoned for thefts at Ipra in Franconia, and at Neuenstatt on the Aysch, yet had never confessed to anything under torture. On this occasion he climbed into his godfather's house and stole two beds, also set fire to the house. Besides he stole a horse from pasture, but had to pay for it, and did the same with an ox; also dredged a fish pond and stole six hundredweight of fish. Both beheaded here as a favour.

198. July 29th. Hans George Schwartzmann of Dörflass near Bayreuth, a tiler, *alias* ' the fat Lanzknecht,' also ' the Black Peasant,' and his wench Anna Pintzrini of Leinpa below

Bamberg ; both thieves, who with a companion climbed into the castle at Greffnberg and stole many articles from the warden ; likewise from the castle at Bischoffa and stole linen ; also at Bamberg from Ruden in his castle and from one of the cathedral clergy there. Committed also many burglaries at the convent of Saint Clare and at that of the Holy Sepulchre. He stole a quantity of silver jewellery from the envoy, Veit Ulrich Marschalt, at his castle ; much silver and linen, with a golden penny having an image on it, from the Dog's Head ; also much gold and clothing from Hans Gossman's castle at Büch. He quarrelled over the share of the booty with his companions at Fischbach, so that they beat him and wounded his wench who helped him. They were caught ; he, Schwartzmann, being hanged as a thief, and his wench beheaded.

These were his associates : Schlot Michael, the ' Scholar of Bareit,' Löffl Kaspar, Kraussberlin (who both wounded him), the ' Scholar Paulus,' Dölp (who was executed), Six and Zulp (these also have since received their due). (*See Part I., No.* 196.)

199. Two thieves hanged.

200. September 2nd. Anna Rebbelin of Pegnitz, who had a house at Aurbach, a thief who entered houses here more than forty times. She went up two or three flights of stairs into the rooms and stole a great quantity of goods. Beheaded with the sword here. (*Note : The executioner bungled his task on this occasion, giving two strokes instead of one.*)

201. A thief hanged.

202. Two male thieves hanged. A female thief beheaded.

203. December 18th. Hermann Wölffel of Neunhof, *alias* the lackey (because he had been the servant of the Margrave) also formerly a butcher; with his associates blackmailed people who visited the prostitutes at Neuenwald, and plundered Jews ; likewise, with his companions, beat a drunken peasant of Dornitz, because he had called him a rogue, so that the man died nine days after. In the affray when he was stabbed at Bruck, he killed a prostitute who had appeared as a witness against him. For these things he was beheaded with the sword at Neucnhoff in the domain of Herr Anthony Geütter. Behaved very wantonly at the end.

204. December 23rd. Cuntz Rhünagel of Dinghoffen, *alias* der Derbss, a farm labourer who threatened the old smith and his son at Ehrabach, and said he would burn their house down, and that he would afterwards cut off their hands and hide them in his breast. Previously he had been whipped out of the town at Forchhaim, because he had tried to break out of prison and had committed some small thefts. Beheaded with the sword here as a favour. At first he refused to receive the sacrament and used abusive language, but afterwards consented.

Total : 15 persons.

Year 1601

205. A murderer beheaded.

206. April 21st. Bastian Grübl of Gumpnhoffen, *alias* der Schlack, a vagabond and thief, who stole much and besides confessed to twenty murders. Among these victims were five pregnant women, whom he had caused to live in debauchery with his companions, then cut them open and cut off the hands of the infants and made candles of their hands to be used in

burglaries. He and his companions also stole children and offered them for sale to the Jews. Lastly also he denounced a farmer's son, little Birger from Clausen, as being one of his associates who had helped him to steal and murder, so that the man was brought into this town and examined by torture in his presence. He did him wrong in this, for he, Birger, had no part in the murder, and the charge was false. Grübl thought that by doing him this injustice the murder would not be discovered, and that he would himself escape by this means ; and he denounced the said Birger only out of enmity. Also Wolff Zerer of Neuendorff, *alias* der Zulp, a thief and beggar, with Anna his mistress, belonging to Neuenmarck, the daughter of a shepherd, who wandered about for seven years with the man Zulp begging and stealing, broke into five churches, one at Goss-manstein and another at Closter Schleisselau, and stole the pyxes and chalices out of them and much besides. For these things the men Schlack and Zulp were hanged here, but Anna beheaded. Nine years ago another paramour of hers, the ' Black Town Beadle,' was executed at Barreuth.

207. May 19th. Hans Taumb, a wire-drawer's son and a soldier who served in five campaigns in Hungary, and Peter Haubmayr of Neuenmarck, also a soldier, who had served in three campaigns in Hungary; both robbers. Taumb, the wire-drawer, had often been in the Beggars' Prison, three times in jail, four times in the cells, and had been condemned for his thefts and crimes and robberies, but reprieved, and also punished in Hungary. Peter too had been reprieved in the same way and punished in Hungary. Both again fell back into their old ways, maintained prostitutes, putting them in the way of people, and if these wished to consort with the women, came out and black-mailed them, taking their money or clothes. For these offences both were beheaded here. The men were associates of ' the lackey ' (*see No. 203*).

208. June 16th. A thief beheaded as a favour, because he had lain long in prison.

209. A thief hanged.

210. Two thieves hanged.

211. October 13th. Lienhardt Leydtner of Rotenburg in Bavaria, a padlock smith ; Luntz

Riegelbauer of Humpfflesshoff, a farm-labourer, both thieves and robbers. In the last two years Leydtner has opened the doors of forty-two shops in this town during the night with keys he has manufactured, thinking to find money, and has obtained some in a few, otherwise has stolen nothing special. Riegelbauer also stole, but in the streets, snatching purses from the girdles of twenty-four women and taking the money. Both hanged here.

212. November 12th. Michael Vogl of Bamberg, a gardener's son, beheaded as a favour here for having killed a *Lanzknecht*. Bartholomew Kreutzer of Presat in the Palatinate, who had also been a robber and had plundered people in company with the man Trodtzieher (already executed) and Haubmayr. In a meadow by the Ochsenbach the *Lanzknecht* quarrelled with him about a robbery they had committed and tried to stab him. Whereupon he, Vogl, seized his gun and shot him, so that he instantly fell dead; and stripped and plundered him, taking 40 florins. He also stole a hose and doublet from Hans Parthl, Rosenau's servant.

Total : 13 persons.

Year 1602

213. January 19th. Hans Fischross of Ecker-
smühl, a weaver and sacristan at Eckelsbuch
and Feucht, who stole candlesticks and chalices
out of the churches and money out of the alms-
boxes. Besides, he stole about four measures
of corn and six pecks of oats at Feucht. Beheaded as a favour. (*Note : The executioner
bungled his work.*)

214. March 13th. Michael Dietmayr, a tailor
of Dippersdorf, who killed with a chopper a
peasant of Weygelshoffn called ' der Lohr.' He
went for a walk with him and gave him a blow
on the head from behind, so that he fell; then
dealt him two more blows. He found 3 florins
3 pfennigs on him, then dragged the body into
a fir wood and left it ; also took some clothes
from his landlord. For these things he was
executed on the wheel at Lauff, where he was
caught.

215. May 20th. Cuntz Heckermann of
Welckendorff above Schesslitz, a trader and a
thief, *alias* fat Küntzla and ' Schandt,' who stole
2,000 florins' worth of chains, rings and silver
jewellery from the dean of the Cathedral (named

Neüstetter) at Bamberg. Also stole many other things besides. Hanged here.

216. September 14th. George Praun of Mannsfeld, a cook and swordsman, who stole 13 dollars from the bag of a youth from Greyffenberg who was travelling with him, putting stones in their place. After that again took 8 florins from him at Koppenhagen ; spent 1 florin of it. Again took 5 florins from him at Hamburg. At Vienna he stole a pair of white silk stockings from a man, and from a Walloon wagon a valise containing a blue mantle and a pair of red velvet hose, also a white satin doublet. Beheaded here. When placed on the stone his head turned several times as if it wanted to look about it, moved its tongue and opened its mouth as if wanting to speak, for a good half quarter of an hour. I have never seen the like of this.

217. A thief and burglar hanged.

218. October 26th. Lienhardt Kopp of Amburg, *alias* the Handsome Fellow, a cooper and *Lanzknecht,* who two years ago stabbed Schnecken Matthew the inn-keeper at Fürth and his wife who was pregnant ; also stabbed the Jew called Mennlein for the sake of a

prostitute over the payment of some liquor (this deed was seen). Beheaded and put on the wheel.

Total : 6 persons.

Year 1603

219. January 18th.   Michael Schober, a hook-maker and son of a burgher here, stole 19 florins from his cousin at Kleinreuth, who refused him when he asked to be boarded in his house. He hid himself and watched until the house was deserted, so that he could creep in by a window and steal the money from a chest.   On the strength of a written communication from his cousin he was whipped out of the town at Schweinitz.   When at large again he hid under a bed in the house of Wagner, who had taught him his trade, and stole about 30 florins.   After obtaining his liberty he was arrested at Lauff for theft.

Hans Marti of Wahmbach, a broom-binder, *alias* Seuhans, a thief of bleached stuffs, who stole from the bleachers at the bleaching grounds of Megeldorff, Upper and Lower Galgenhoff, and Tafflhoff.

Schober was beheaded by favour ; Marti was hanged, and the bleachers made him a pair of very white hose, a doublet and stockings of Cologne linen. He was delivered up at Forchheim.

220. Two thieves hanged.

221. May 7th. Matthew Stertz of Grüntling, a soldier who had served in five campaigns, stabbed a ditcher of Aylsdorf near the Rabenstein because he is said to have begged of him; and when the burgomaster spoke to him, asking why he had so wounded him, he stabbed at him also ; went afterwards into the city and asked to be tried. Had been a Catholic, but turned Lutheran. Beheaded at Aylsdorf.

222. May 27th. Cuntz Neuner, *alias* Heintzl Cuntz, of Perngau, who twelve years ago, on account of some pigeons taken from him, and being also drunk, in his fury set fire to and burnt down his house and helped to extinguish the fire with others. Then three years ago he stole to the value of 60 florins from one of his friends at Perngau, and when the latter thrashed him for it he threatened to burn his house, so that the friend had to agree to pay 50 florins besides.

He also threatened to burn the house of one of his friends who had brought up his young daughter in his house for four years, if he did not give her some wages ; then also threatened one of his friends at the Rockstock, from whom he had stolen a cow and who had recovered it, that if he did not give him 15 florins he would burn down his house and farm so that it could be swept up with a broom afterwards. Lastly he stole much in the way of bedclothes and corn at different times. For these crimes he was beheaded as a favour at Saltzberg.

223. October 11th. Lienhardt Taller, *alias* Spisslindl, of Greussberg, a peasant who bought oxen in the presence of the market overseer and remained in debt to the amount of 50 florins. When a messenger was sent to fetch the money, he gave it to him, and as the latter, who spent the night with him, was lying upon a chest and talking to him, he seized an axe from the wall and dealt him two blows on the head, killing him immediately. He then took back the money, hid the body under some straw in a shed, hanged his dog and killed it and burned it there. On the next night, with the help of his wife, he carried

out the man's body to a little wood and buried
it. This murder was committed a year and a
half ago. He was arrested for this at Aylsdorf,
brought in to this town and executed on the
wheel.

224. A thief beheaded as a favour.

Total : 8 persons.

Year 1604

225. March 6th. Peter Hoffmann of Bamberg,
who had been twice banished the town for thefts,
again broke into many gardens and stole vegetables, doing much damage besides. Also broke
open beehives, let himself down into the town
moat near the Haller postern and stole the
copper buckets there ; also deserted his wife and
took a mistress ; then, when she died, took
another and had the banns published at Lauff.
Beheaded here as a favour.

226. June 16th. George Mayr of Lower Riss-
bach, a beggar and thief who stole many things
at various times ; hanged at Liechtenau. Was
17 years old, and had begun to steal at the
age of eight.

227. August 13th.   Michael Seydel of Middle
Erabach, a shoemaker's journeyman, who,
breaking through a wall by night, entered the
house of his grandfather's brother, a joiner, and
inflicted thirty-eight wounds on his head with
a jagged stone, and one in the neck with a shoemaker's knife, intending to cut his throat and
take his money.   Beheaded on a scaffold at
Greffenberg, the joiner dying also in the same
quarter of an hour.   No one had been executed
in the town for 106 years.

228. September 15th.   Cuntz Pütner of Upper
Reith, Master Fürer's shepherd, and Hans
Drentz of Petzhoffn, *alias* ' the finch ' and ' the
long one,' both thieves.   The shepherd had twice
concealed himself in Master Fürer's house and
tried to break into the office and steal money,
but when he had bored seven holes the first time
he effected nothing ;   had also stolen 54 florins
from his master Schmaltzig at Herspruck.
Drintz, ' the long one,' had been whipped out of
Presat once and had twice broken out of jail ;
had stolen much also.   Both were hanged at
Herspruck.   The shepherd died as a Christian,
but ' the long one ' would not pray or say a word

about God, nor confess the name of Christ. When questioned about God he always said he knew nothing about Him, and could say nothing nor repeat any prayer. A young girl had once given him a shirt and since then he had been unable to pray. The sacrament was not administered to him, therefore he died in his sins. He fell down near the gallows as if tormented by a fit ; he was a godless man.

229. September 18th. Elizabeth Püffin, daughter of a citizen and a serving maid, who, entering the Keeper's house at Velden where she was in service, and then the room of his brother-in-law, a gouty old man, dealt him about eleven wounds on the head with a bar, nearly cutting one of his arms in two. Then, thinking he was dead, she opened the press, took the money and made off. When she was arrested at Neühaus and brought here she obtained a respite of 32 weeks on the plea of pregnancy, the committee of sworn women visiting her 18 times. She confessed also that she had robbed the butcher Schwander of much, to the value of 60 florins in the way of clothes alone. Beheaded with the sword as a favour. Behaved in a Christian way.

230. October 13th.   Conrad Zwickelsperger, burgher and compass-maker of this town, because of his immoral relations with Barbara Wagnerin, a carpenter's wife (which, however, began before he had a wife and she a husband).   Three times he prompted the woman to put insect-powder in her husband's food.   This she did, putting it in some porridge and even eating three spoonfuls herself; which powder did not harm the man; he vomited six times and she twice, for, as Zwickel had told her, if she gave him too much he would die, if little he would only vomit.   Zwickel also pledged himself by going to communion not to have intimacy with any other woman than with her, the carpenter's wife, and she was to go and promise him the same.   Also the man Zwickel gave two florins to an old witch that she might cause the carpenter to be stabbed, struck down, or drowned.   In the same way he had had immoral relations with the mother of the carpenter's wife twenty-four years before, and also with three sisters called Pfisterin, as well as with other married women. For these crimes he was beheaded as a favour and his body burnt.

231. October 30th. Barbara Wagnerin, the mistress of Conrad Zwickel, because she gave her husband, Lienhardt Wagner, a carpenter, insect-powder in porridge to eat, eating three spoonfuls of it herself, and also had immoral relations with eighteen married men and bachelors. Beheaded with the sword as a favour. (*See Part I., No. 230.*)

Total : 6 persons.

Year 1605

232. A thief beheaded.

233. May 2nd. Hans Paier of Aylsdorf, a *lanzknecht*, son of the old town-beadle and who had served in three campaigns in Hungary, also Hans Rühl of Nuremberg, a cloth dresser and knacker. Because of three of his robberies, committed against men who visited the prostitutes in the Neuenwald, where he blackmailed, plundered and robbed them of their money with the help of his companion, Paier should have been executed and his life forfeited, but his life was granted him by request on the day of his trial. Condemned to 10 years' at the

frontier house in Hungary ; never went there however ; but again robbed two people with the help of his companion, of which robbery his share was 5 orts ($1\frac{1}{4}$ guldens). In the Palatinate he and his associates, fifteen in number, seized eight cloaks belonging to eight Anabaptists, sold and disposed of them. Rühl on the other hand, a few years ago, while yet a boy, killed another boy of ten by throwing a stone at him, and was sent to prison for it. When he obtained his freedom he consorted with the knacker, was banished from the town for his evil ways, and has now killed another man. Both beheaded with the sword by favour here at Nuremberg.

234. A thief hanged.

235. July 9th. Hans Grosselfinger, a carpenter, who had worked for Master Peundt for twenty-four years and who was a pensioner and sacristan at the almshouse here for four years and was seventy-five years old, without any cause stabbed with a knife another pensioner, a carpenter called Moller, also aged about eighty. Beheaded with the sword here for this.

236. July 23rd. Barbara Zeylerin of Hohen-hasslach, residing at Feldorff in the Palatinate, married and had borne five children, who had immoral relations with Endrass Heroldt at Herspruck twelve years ago, and, recently, also with a father and his son, a rich peasant, with the father many times in eight years, with the son thrice in one year, father and son being, however, unaware of each other's doings. Beheaded with the sword here as a favour.

237. December 23rd (a Monday). Master Doctor Nicholas von Gilgen, who was by appointment a privy councillor in an honourable council and was bound to that council by oaths he did not observe; for the sake of money received wrote for and advised two (opposite) parties in many affairs; also gave evidence and sat in council for deliberations and decisions; also stole from my lords of this town the allowances for beer and wine, causing it to be stored by his servants. Also he debauched before her marriage, forcing her to do his will, his servant whom he brought from Trier to this town, and whom he gave as a wife to his clerk Philip Tümbler, by a promise of 50 florins and

large presents. According to her declaration she brought forth five children by him, three of which miscarried during delivery or by fright in the twelfth week, two remaining alive, a boy and girl, he being sponsor to the boy at baptism. Similarly, by like promises, he forced his under-maid to consent to his will a year ago, and tried likewise to persuade his brother's two daughters; one, the wife of Doctor Wurffbaum, he tried to compel, but she resisted, the other the wife of Doctor Calrot, who yielded to his will and consorted with him before and after her marriage, according to her account through fear and compulsion and the promise of many presents and a wedding portion (he did not admit he compelled her, and I do not believe he forced her).

Lastly he played false when serving the Prince of Sultzbach, whose advocate he was; he also mediated dishonestly between the families of Nuremberg, and between the noble families of Leschwitz and Redwitz, writing to, and advising both parties in one affair. Likewise he counselled the Italian Charles Albert Nello and other Italians against the rulers of our town ; also stole the decrees from the office of an honourable councillor. In Italy too, at Padua, he produced a false certificate, when he figured as a doctor there by means of a false certificate, for he became a doctor at Basel only long after. For his evil deeds he lay in prison for thirty-eight weeks in Lugins Land and in the jail. He was led out on Monday by favour in a long mourning cloak, his arms bound behind him with a black silk cord, and led by a cord, a black cloth being spread on the seat (on the scaffold). When he had been beheaded his body was wrapped in the cloth and laid in a wooden coffin, nailed down and taken to St. Peter's church by the assistant executioner, but removed at night in a cart to St. John's by the little gate that leads to the Butts, and buried in the graveyard by the walls.

Total : 6 persons.

Year 1606

238. March 4th. George and Nicholas Widtmann, brothers, sons of a carpenter, who at various times stole many cloaks, hats, tin and

copper vessels out of houses. They should have been executed two and a half years ago, for they had been condemned to death but were reprieved. Often lay in hospital; now hanged at the new place of execution.

239. May 17th. Dorothea Meulin of Fischstain, a country girl who gave birth to a child two years ago, fourteen days before Candlemas, at night, in the garden of her employer, a farmer at Obernhaydelbach. She stopped its mouth with earth, and making a hole with her hand, buried it while it was still struggling. Recently gave birth to another child in a cow-shed and hid it under the straw, thinking to smother it, but the farmer's wife arrived, found it, and rescued it. Beheaded with the sword for these crimes at Aylsdorf.

240. June 26th. Susannah Ritlin of Regenstauff, a servant, who had a child by a nailmaker. When she gave birth to it secretly she wrung its little neck, put it in a pot and threw it down a privy and into the river Pegnitz. Beheaded here as a favour.

241. July 2nd. Laurence Schropp, a miller's man of Liechtenau, who worked for 22 years at

his cousin's mill and stole corn from him, ground it and offered it for sale to the peasants. By his account he only gained about 400 florins. Beheaded here as a favour.

242. August 11th. A peasant of Grundtla who killed two peasants with an axe, spared by petition.

Total : 5 persons.

Year 1607

243. June 11th. Veit Fladen of Etzelsau, belonging to the district of Liechtenau, a poacher, who carried on his poaching for about three years. He shot point-blank through coat and holsters at a mounted man near Allmussen, whom he took for a gamekeeper, and did the same to one of the Margrave's keepers whose horse he shot ; also beat Wallet Sauer unmercifully, taking him for a spy on poachers. Beheaded with the sword here for these crimes.

244. August 4th. Margaret Marranti, a country girl from the knackers' sheds, who was in service with the innkeeper there, had intercourse with a carrier whom she did not know,

and became pregnant. Took service with the farmer at Dörrenhof at Candlemas, concealing her pregnancy. When she was haymaking in the meadows, was seized with pains and contortions, and when the farmer's wife said she would send for the midwife, the girl made an excuse, and remaining behind at night, gave birth to a child near a shed by the river Pegnitz. She immediately threw the child into the water and drowned it, though it stirred and struggled. Beheaded with the sword here on this account.

Total : 2 persons.

Year 1608

245. October 11th. Hans Neubaur of Rötenbach, who stabbed the Forester at Eyba with a halberd through a window. He had frequented the courts at Anspach and had a safe-conduct. The affair arose from a quarrel in a wood about a cart-horse ; the forester had seized it and taken it as a pledge, but gave it back. When Neubaur paid for their drinks at the tavern, the forester would not be satisfied with a florin's worth, and thus it came to a quarrel.

246. A thief beheaded as a favour.

247. December 6th. Ulrich Bömer of Kruppach, a thief who stole five cows and also helped to rob three peasants—six florins from one at the Three Firs, two florins from another at the Oven Fork, and seven from another at Röttenbach by Lauff ; also married two wives. Arrested at Aylsdorf ; hanged here.

Total : 3 persons.

Year 1609

248. February 10th. Hans Fratzn from Franconia, who had been a town guard here, a thief who stole ten bed blankets about eighteen weeks ago and broke into the ' Huder ' at Bamberg, stealing about 30 florins' worth of clothes. Caught in the act of stealing from a bed at Heroltzberg, where Master Jacob Geutter had him beheaded as a favour.

249. March 9th. Hans Schrenker, *alias* der Hotsch, of Drossendorf near Holffelt, a cooper and thief who climbed into the castle at Freienfels, first by means of a ladder over the cowshed, then by a ladder against a tower to the

roof, then again by another ladder through a window into a room. Broke open a press with his cooper's knife and stole about 300 florins' worth of silver jewellery, then descending by the ladders as he had climbed, went out in front of the castle and hid the jewels under a stone on the other side of the hill. Entered again by the ladders, broke open a table and stole a bag with 40 florins, although a bag with 500 florins lay close to it. When he was about to take the money, his courage failed and he ran away, thinking for certain that someone was running after him. All this happened three years ago. He was brought into Lauff on a litter and was hanged here. Did not receive communion; he was a Catholic and thought he should be allowed to go on a pilgrimage to Lassen to his confessor, after which he would return. Said and did many strange things when he was led out, declaring too that if they hanged him he would quickly take from his bag a knife which he kept hidden, and cut himself down and run away; but nothing came of it.

250. Two men beheaded for stabbing others in a quarrel.

251. December 7th. Fritz Carel of Megelsdorf, a ditcher, because he stole eleven pieces of stuff from Fuchsen the bleacher here at the fulling and bleaching place, and because the bleacher feared he might set fire to his works. Beheaded with the sword here ; he was seventy-five years old.

Total : 5 persons.

Year 1610

252. January 23rd. Maria Cordula Hunnerin of Weidenberg, a weaver's daughter, who stole clothes from her mistress at Bamberg a year ago with the help of another maid, and was banished from our territory. Later she took up with a cloth manufacturer's son at Aylsdorf, and giving herself out to be the daughter of the innkeeper at the Black Bear in Bayreuth, hired a carriage, drove to the inn there with her betrothed and a soldier's wife, ordered food and drink to be prepared, pointed out an old man as her father, and offered to fetch her sister. Then, after having eaten and drunk for a while she departed, leaving the others

sitting in the inn, and the soldier's wife had to pay 32 florins. Later on she stole 800 florins' worth in dollars, other coin, and three-kreutzer pieces from her master the town-smith, in whose house she had served for half a year. Caught at Lauff and beheaded here with the sword.

253. March 15th. Hans Körnmayer of Nuremberg, *alias* Hannamann, who had learnt the trade of compass-making and then of cloth dyeing with Rinderer, who discharged him and had him imprisoned for having robbed him. Because of this happening he departed for half a year, came back, entered the house, remained there overnight and took 9 pewter dishes, an old cloak, 7 ells of white stuff, 2 lbs. of Brazil-wood, 6 lbs. of deer's tallow, a ham, two pairs of stockings, also made a hole in a cupboard, but took nothing. He pawned all these things to a Jew at Fürth for 7½ florins. Previously he had stolen about a hundredweight of tartar, and sold it for 7½ florins to pay for his board. Rinderer had him brought in as a prisoner, and he was beheaded with the sword as a favour.

254. November 6th. Magdalen Fischerin of

Culmbach, daughter of 'Black' Merden, an unmarried servant who lost her maidenhood by a *Lanzknecht* five years ago, served at the ringmaker Fürheller's house in the Kreuzgasse, and had a child by father and son. Beheaded with the sword here as a favour.

Total: 3 persons.

Year 1611

255. A thief, not hanged but beheaded as a favour.

256. January 22nd. George Egloff of Culmbach, living in the Affiertal, a carpenter, who prepensely killed his apprentice with an axe in a beech wood (he owed him 9 florins). Arrested at Eschenau and beheaded with the sword here at Nuremberg by favour (instead of being hanged).

257. February 28th. Elizabeth Mechtlin, called by her father's name, wife of Christopher Sahr, a confectioner in the Wine Market, who betrayed her husband three times, but was taken back again by him. Lastly she went away with a man, then lived about as a common

prostitute ; also committed lewdness with two brothers, Hannssen Schneider, confectioners, among the butchers' stalls. Beheaded with the sword as a favour instead of being hanged. (*Note : the execution was bungled.*)

258. March 5th. Philip Lohner of Hilperstein, a pedlar, and Cunigund Küplin, a shepherdess at Rückersdorff. Lohner committed lewdness with her and her daughter ; took the mother in marriage first, then let her go and took the daughter. Later he let her go also, and took back the mother, both women consenting to this. The two beheaded with the sword here as a favour, and both bodies afterwards burnt.

259. March 12th. Hans Wunderer of Immeldorf, a bridlemaker and poacher, who shot the gamekeeper at Hirsbrun and split his head with a chopper. Beheaded here with the sword, as a favour.

260. Two thieves hanged.

261. A thief—not hanged but beheaded as a favour.

262. September 26th. Heuckelsperger, a butcher of Lantzhüt, residing at Lichtenau,

broke into the house of a butcher at Wehr with Dieterich; he stole first 27 florins, then 64 florins, and the third time ⅝ of a hundredweight of tallow from a locksmith in Beckschlager street, and always committed thefts when he came here from Liechtenau.

Margaret Wagnerin of Feucht, a common prostitute, who for about 20 years has haunted the Neuenwald, also called ' the peasant's girl,' committed lewdness with men and youths, accused some who were innocent, stole money from their breeches' pockets; often taken into Carolsburg and severely chastised ; as a favour she was beheaded, but the butcher was hanged.

263. A thief hanged.

Total : 12 persons.

Year 1612

264. A thief hanged.

265. March 5th. Michael Gemperlein of Micheldorf, a butcher and *Lanzknecht*, a murderer, robber and thief, who three years ago should have been hanged for theft but was reprieved. Now murdered with an axe by night, in a shed

at an inn in Neunkirchen in the Palatinate, a *Lanzknecht* and his wife, which man was a cooper at Guntznhausen, the woman being, it was supposed, pregnant ; also took 3½ florins and their clothes, together with the weapon. Likewise he took 30 florins from a carter at Bayrsdorf, then took clothes and linen from an old man at Lohnersdorf and killed him in his bed ; killed a messenger at Regensburg and took 150 florins. Item: killed a bargeman at Linz, taking 70 florins and throwing the body into the Danube ; took 30 florins from a man in the Böhmerwald and wounded him grievously ; took 20 florins from a man at Eger and wounded him ; knocked a carter from his horse with an axe in the Erlanger wood, so that he lay as if dead, and took 75 florins from him ; took 24 florins from a messenger there, and committed besides many highway robberies and thefts. For these things he was led out in a cart, had his body torn four times with red-hot tongs, and was then executed on the wheel. Had many confederates.

266. June 2nd. Kunz Höffler of Zeyern, a butcher, *alias* Bengelholtz, who attacked a

carrier of Amburg by night in the Laufferwald near Bergnersdorf, inflicted seven wounds on him and took 5 orths from his purse, broke open his packages and took the wares from them, and gave the stolen goods into the keeping of a companion, in whose house they were found. Beheaded with the sword here for this.

267. June 23rd. Andrew Feuerstein, who kept a school with his father; debauched sixteen schoolgirls. Beheaded as a favour instead of being hanged.

268. A thief hanged.

269. August 4th. Matthew Werdtfritzn of Fürth, a *Lanzknecht, alias* ' Eightfingers,' a robber. With the help of a companion he attacked the carrier from Regensburg in the Neuenwald, wounded him and his son mortally, and took about 800 florins' worth of money and goods. Took 84 florins from the baker woman of Lauff, and wounded her lad in the same way, so that he was thought likely to die. Took 40 florins from a carter and 18 florins from the fisherman of Fach ; in all twelve highway robberies. For these crimes he was executed on the wheel as a robber.

270. October 1st. Laurence Stollman of Culmbach, from the Wolfsgorge, a coach-boy and
thief who stole 150 florins out of a coach from
a man (this money was again stolen from him
at Staffelstein). Stole many things besides.
As he had not enjoyed the proceeds of his theft,
he was beheaded as a favour.

271. December 3rd. Nicholas Müllner, of Nor-
thausen, a vagabond and thief who entered
the house of the innkeeper of Schur through
the cellar, and was caught. Stole many things
at various times in his home district ; hanged
here.

272. December 17th. Bartholomew Deigela,
a barber and son of a citizen of this town, who
snatched their cloaks from people by night in
the streets, took five of them and two from
women ; beheaded here as a favour and not
hanged. (*Note : the execution was bungled.*)

Total : 9 persons.

Year 1613

273. January 28th. George Mertz of Letten,
alias der Schlegel, a thief, lived in Gigentzenhoff,

who stole many things in seventy-two villages—
hanged. Behaved queerly as he was led out,
shook his head and only laughed, would not
pray, only said that his faith had helped him.

274. July 8th. George Prückner, a citizen
of this town and a cooper's son, who was a
very bad character ; had been several times
imprisoned in the tower, but was liberated on
promise of amendment. Broke out of prison
at Schnaydta, broke into a shop full of embroidered stockings in the Market Place, pawned
them, besides stole 8 ducats from a carrier,
which he had to restore. Stole again from
another carrier 5 florins and a mantle. When in
prison he gave out that he had received from
the night watchman at Kreimbs something
against wounds which he must eat, having
promised in return, however, never to think of
God nor pray to Him. This he ate, and said
he had sold himself to the devil ; and indeed he
tried to break out and behaved wantonly, as
if the evil spirit tormented him.

When he was reprieved and shut up in the
tower as a punishment, he twice broke thick
irons during the first two nights and pulled out

nails as long as a finger, and when he was secured with four chains he broke them, so that one of our worthy councillors caused him to be put back into the town prison and, no betterment being probable, had him beheaded as a favour, because he had become converted. He behaved in Christian fashion in the end.

275. July 13th. Sebastian Bernecker, son of a locksmith and citizen, stole the corn from the bakers' corn bins, breaking into them several times, opening five locks on one, and three on the other, and locking them again after. By his own account he stole as much as 70 florins' worth in seven weeks, but by the bakers' calculation far above 100 florins' worth. Beheaded with the sword as a favour.

Total : 5 persons.

Year 1614

276. January 25th. Hans Ulerich of Heroltz-berg, *alias* Cuntz Bauer, who had been in prison and also been banished from the town for theft. Benedict Fellbinger of Allersbach, called ' the Devil's lad,' who had also been in jail and

lain fifteen times in the town cells, who broke his ban eleven times—both of them thieves who stole many things at various times. Beheaded with the sword here as a favour, instead of being hanged.

277. February 8th. Anna Emblin of Amburg, a glazier's daughter who bore a child to a jeweller's workman. The child was born alive ; she held it up by the arm for a quarter of an hour, and when it struggled she thrust it alive into the privy. Beheaded with the sword here.

278. March 8th. Elizabeth Birckelin of Hirschbach, who, because her father George Birckel, a barber-surgeon of that town and a very wicked man, treated her harshly, gave him about 4 lbs. (?) of insect-powder to eat in some vegetables, on the chance of his dying at once. As he vomited it and fell sick, she sent for 1 oz. of Magovium and intended to use it, but this became known. She also stole great sums of money from him to give to her betrothed, who was a papermaker. Beheaded with the sword, not hanged, as a favour.

279. March 10th. Hans Ditz of Frankfort, a slater, *alias* Henssa von Frankfurt, who picked

men's pockets to the tune of 66 purses, and stabbed his father-in-law so that he died after 10 weeks. There were 746 florins in the purses. Beheaded, and not hanged, as a favour. He sang all the way when he went to his death.

280. June 28th. Hans Brunnauer, a clerk who, during his wife's lifetime, committed lewdness with Barbara Kettner, during her husband's life; promised her marriage, consorted with her for three years, went about the country with her for half a year, and had a child by her. Similarly he consorted twice with the woman Kettner's sister, and several times with the stepmother of these two women ; so also he boarded and slept with the joiner's wife, known as the woman Thomas, for half a year, and promised her marriage ; also had twin children by a servant during his wife's lifetime. For these things he was beheaded with the sword here, as a favour.

281. July 12th. Conrad Krafft of Eschenau, but lately resident in Filseck, who was a clerk of the law courts for 17 years at Raittlsdorff, 3 years at Bamberg, 6 years at Filseck ; obtained

500 florins' worth of leather from the Austrians. He gave himself out to be a citizen of Forchhaim, saying the town council of Forchhaim would be surety for him and he would bring papers. He then produced two documents, according to which a cloth shearer, called Hans von Forchhaimb, had been stabbed near Vienna and had written to his friends through the judge to come and fetch the property he left; the other document from Weisenburg whereby the wife deputed a man (then in service at the Star Inn at Forchhaim) to fetch it away. So with false seals and documents from the authorities at Forchhaim, in which he appeared as Christopher Kinnbarth, he was able to fetch away the leather.

Secondly he fraudulently obtained two papers in the name of the town council of Colmutz, near Regensburg, pretending that a shoemaker, a native of Colmutz, had been stabbed near Linz, and demanded the property left by the man. When he produced the two documents he gave himself out to be a councillor of Colmutz and fraudulently received 500 florins from the treasurer at Amburg. Likewise, during his service at Bamberg, Raitelsdorf and Filseck he swindled the children over the accounts of wardship, of 50, 30 and 40 florins. For these things he was beheaded here with the sword.

282. July 19th. Hans Drichsler of Bayreuth, *alias* der Birger, or Lanzknecht Hans, a thief who, together with the stonemason Wöllfla, since executed, climbed into Werdamann's house and stole many things. Similarly he broke into the eight shops in the Pig Market, and into various shops elsewhere. Hanged here for these things.

283. October 25th. Andrew Muss and Hans Dorsch, both from Stadt Kranach, sons of brother and sister and (so) cousins. Dorsch served five years with Master Busenreuter, and his cousin Muss taught him to rob; which he did, taking about 1,500 florins from his master ; all of which he did not for Muss only, but for young Schweyckert and a barber's man called Jacob, for a tailor called der Schmied, for a maid called Merckel, another maid called Elss, and recently a compass-maker called der Hyrn. He also committed lewdness with them. For these things both were beheaded with the

sword as a special favour, on the Outer Rabenstein.

Total : 10 persons.

Year 1615

284. January 12th. Balthasar Preyss, son of
a citizen of this town, a thief who was eleven
times in the cells, went several times to jail,
was for half a year in the Frog Tower, half a
year in irons in the Tower, but would not
abandon thieving ; and because he was put
to some handicraft, ran away and stole. Beheaded with the sword for this as a favour, and
not hanged.

285. February 28th. Michael Willet of Gün-
tersbühl, a day-labourer who stole many things
with the man Hans Hacken ; also informed
against poachers. Lately, however, he and a
companion called Andrew met a goose-herd
and his young son in the wood near Leinberg.
Andrew attacked him, and taking his musket-
rest, struck him on the head, then he, Willet,
struck him on the back twice with an axe he
had with him, and then caught the boy and

threatened to kill him if he cried out. But Andrew took the axe from him and struck the goose-herd on the head so many times that he lay as dead, and took 9 florins in money—the goose-herd dying after two hours. Executed on the wheel here for this crime.

286. March 7th.   Margaret Lindtnery of Schnabelweydt, who bore a child to a shoe-maker. It was born secretly at her master's (a ropemaker) house in St. John's Street. She smothered it and pushed it into a pot, and afterwards throttled it. Beheaded with the sword here.

287. March 21st.   Laurence Demer, of Rit-tling on the Aysch, near Neuenstadt, *alias* ' the long peasant,' a thief who stole much at various times by burglary. Hanged here; was two fingers less than three ells in height.

288. May 23rd.   Caspar Frantz of Sunac-heim, living at Otingen, a servant of Lord Heroldt, from whose cupboard he took the key, opened his iron trunk, stole 170 florins out of it in two visits, and squandered all but 100 florins. Beheaded with the sword as a favour.

289. June 22nd.   Lienhardt Müller, a butcher,

alias Scheidlein, who stole many household articles, also tin, copper, and sheep. Beheaded with the sword here as a favour. The ladder was already placed against the gallows, but he was spared (hanging) and executed near the timber stacks.

290. November 2nd. Hans Ziegler of Brodt, *alias* der Botz, who threatened to burn down the houses of his friends and guardians for refusing him money, though he had formerly squandered it on women and prostitutes. Beheaded with the sword, as a favour.

291. December 7th. Hans Raim of Elsheim, an embosser in the new hospital, beheaded with the sword here, as a favour, and exposed on the wheel for a murderous assault committed on a woman behind Fischbach. He thought he had killed her; and he found 5 orts (1¼ guldens) on her.

292. December 14th. Michael König, son of a nail-maker; was a burgher residing here at Wehr, who stole many things at various times. The ladder was already resting against the gallows for him, but he was beheaded with the sword as a favour, close to the gallows.

293. December 19th. Five young men hanged,

who had stolen many things at various times :
a peasant, a shoemaker and cobbler, a tan-
ner of white leather, a son of one of the
town-guard, a tailor and weaver. All five
swung from one beam. Four priests were with
them, two from St. Sebald's Church, Master
Hagendorn and Master Wolfgang Lutherer,
besides two of St. Laurence Church, Master
Singer and Master Ernst. Five town-beadles rode
with them, for there was a great throng of people.

Total : 14 persons.

Year 1616

294. January 16th. Two women led out on
a cart. One was the maid who was a servant
of young Mistress von Ploben. She attacked
her mistress and murdered her in bed by night
in her sleep. For this she was twice nipped
with red-hot tongs in each arm, as she was
led out on the cart ; then her head was struck off
and fixed on the gallows and her body thrown
into the pit. The other was a cooper's wife
whose husband committed a murder and ran
away ; but she helped in stealing and carrying

off the goods. Beheaded also and buried—
it was snowing heavily.

295. March 22nd. Leonard Deüerlein, a
cooper's man of Kaltreüth, an audacious knave,
executed because he threatened and warned
people he would burn their houses down. When
his sentence was read to him he said he was
willing to die, but asked as a favour that he
should be allowed to fence and fight with four
of the guards; his request was refused.

296. A thief hanged.

Total : 4 persons.

Year 1617

297. March 20th. Benedict N. called Schinbein, who lived by stealing and other evil doings.
Was the son of a citizen and took to a vagrant life
in various parts ; lived about here in St. John's
quarter, and made a living at the gambling
houses. Beheaded with the sword as a favour.

298. June 26th. —— a bookbinder who stole
more than 300 florins' worth of goods from his
master. Besides, he entered houses by night
at various times and stole tin, copper, clothes,

cloaks, meat, which he disposed of afterwards. The ladder was already placed against the gallows for him, but he was beheaded as a favour, by the timber stacks.

299. September 11th. Two citizens, here; one, a wire-drawer called Kepla, quite ruined the iron merchant Barthel Kostert by his thefts, for he entered his warehouse by night and locked it after him again, so that no one saw or watched him. He stole iron wire and steel nails in considerable quantities, causing the goods to be hawked and sold among the workpeople by his wife and children; he also dealt in false coin. The other, a gardener and regular carrier and messenger, called 'the cabbage grower,' who was entrusted with money several times and often found untrustworthy, lately ventured on a good trick. Knowing that he was carrying to Frankfort some silver jewellery and money, which he had received here from worthy Master Rosenthaler and for which he was responsible, he opened the parcel, sold some of the contents, wasted the money in eating and gambling, then made himself scarce. But at last news was received that he was

living in foreign territory. He was brought in here through one of the honourable councillors. Both men hanged.

300. November 13th. Burnt alive here a miller of Manberna, who however was lately engaged as a carrier of wine, because he and his brother, with the help of others, practised coining and counterfeiting money and clipping coins fraudulently; he had also a knowledge of magic. His brother escaped from the mill, and the Margrave locked the place up and con- fiscated the property. A certain Zachariah, a farrier and 'scutcheon-maker, called 'the heralds-smith,' was mixed up in this; also a file-cutter living in the Bretterne Meer quarter, called 'Karl the file-cutter.' He had a familiar spirit and was a lying knave. These two escaped. This miller, who worked in the town mills here three years ago, fell into the town moat on Whitsunday. It would have been better for him if he had been drowned, but it turned out according to the proverb that 'What belongs to the gallows cannot drown in water.'

This was the last person whom I, Master Franz, executed.

PART II
MINOR BODILY PUNISHMENTS
(Selected)

MINOR BODILY PUNISHMENTS

Year 1583

63. January 10th. Mary Kürssnerin, a young prostitute, who was a watchman's (? musketeer's) daughter, a girl who had thieved considerably and a handsome young creature with whom the young Dietherr had dealings ; Elizabeth Gütlerin, a bath attendant ; Katherine Aynerin, *alias* die Gescheydin, a blacksmith's wife and a handsome creature ; all three children of citizens, and prostitutes, were here pilloried and afterwards flogged out of the town. Such a dreadful crowd ran out to see this that several people were crushed to death under the Frauenthor. Subsequently Mary's ears were cut off, and she was hanged. (*See Part I., No. 77.*)

Year 1584

81. July 4th. Jerome Beyhlstein, a citizen ; because he had taken money for allowing his wife to be unchaste, and because, by prostituting

her, he had acted as procurer and had thereby obtained money, food, and drink ; and whenever anyone had been with her, Beyhlstein had sent a bill round to the man's house and received the fee. He was lashed out of the town, and his wife subsequently executed.

Year 1585

97. July 15th. Barbara Ludtwigin, wife of the barber Maurier (in the Lauffer Square) a housewife ; because before and after marriage she had been incontinent with six people. She had also blasphemed so horribly against the Almighty that a galley and two small ships besides could have been filled with her profanity. Whipped out of this place. (She had two razors about her and intended to murder her husband.) Also pilloried.

Year 1586

118. November 26th. The Shepherd of Weyr because for the last two years he had played the ghost in the house, and tugged at people's feet or heads in their sleep. By this means he

contrived to have connection with the peasant's daughter. Flogged out of the place.

Year 1587

121. January 19th. Heintz Zetzmann of Heuchling, a thief who had given out that he was going to the Venusberg, and knew where the treasure was lying hidden, and how that the Devil had twice given him money on the stone bridge above Lauff. Nothing of which had happened, but he had stolen money and much besides. Flogged out of the town.

126. April 20th. Sarah, a baker's wife of Fach, daughter of the landlord at Halssbronner's Hoff; because she had allowed her maid to be incontinent. She had also incited a smith to force the maid to lechery; on which account, she was, as a favour, merely lashed out of the town.

Year 1588

142. April 27th. Linhardt Mülner, innkeeper at Hambach, because out of insolence and wantonness he had wounded people in the street. Whipped out of Herspruck.

157. December 13th. Ann Pergmennin, of Wolffslohe, a thief, who had crept into a schoolmaster's house near the church of St. Lawrence with intent to steal, but was driven out and caught. A week before she had got herself locked in Hans Payrn's cellar for the purpose of robbery. When she was captured she gave out that she would ride off on a pitchfork along with a besom-binder; but nothing of the kind happened. For which things she was whipped out of the town.

Year 1591

169. April 19th. Andrew Brunner, a citizen and glass worker of Ayldorff, who, during a great storm when it was thundering loudly, blasphemed and railed against the Almighty, called him an old Rascal, said that the old Fool had gambled away his money and lost it at cards, and now wished to win it back by playing at bowls. He also blasphemed violently in other ways, and, as a favour, was stood for one quarter of an hour in the pillory. A piece of his tongue was torn from him on the Fleischbrücke.

Year 1592

175. March 8th.   Hans Gessert of Ritzing, a
weaver and cheating gambler who at back-
gammon, and with the three and five pebbles
had won four dollars from people ; moreover he
had dropped a gilt pfennig before people who
were going by ; and one of these having
picked it up, he sold it to the man for half
(of its supposed) value.   Flogged out of the
town.

179. July 6th.   Dorothy Hoffmennin of Birg,
had given birth to a child at the farm of her employer.   This child she threw into a fishpond,
but, in her confession under torture, said it was
stillborn ; adding that the day before the birth
she had baked, and when mixing the dough
found her pains come on her.   When, however,
the dead child was brought before her and she
was ordered to lay her hands on its head, she
did so with a trembling heart.   A red spot of
blood formed on the place she touched.   By
special favour, she was merely flogged out of
the town.

180. July 10th.   Julius Rühnradt, a baptized
Jew from the Hesse district, to whom the bishop

of Würzburg Julius Echter, and Count Conrad
of Schwartzenburg had stood as sponsors, and
Anna Maria Schwerdtmennin von Weyssmann,
a common prostitute. She had taken up with
the aforesaid Jew, fornicated with him before
and after his baptism, and now purposed to
marry him, although he already had a Jewish
wife, and wished to keep a tavern with another
Jewess. Both flogged out of the town. (*See
Part II., No. 192.*)

Year 1593

188. On the 23rd of August Margaret
Stainla of Offenhausen, otherwise known as
the Spilkundl, who had broken the Ban eight
times, had her fingers cut off. On October
30th, 1590 she had been flogged out of the
town.

189. August 27th. Adam Tupler a carrier
from the Wirtenberg country, to whom Strobl
entrusted a barrel full of old brass, inside which
230 florins were packed. He broke the barrel
open in a wood near Geysslingen, took 111
florins, bought a horse with 35 of these, and

left the remainder of them in the care of the inn-keeper. The remaining 119 florins and the brass he buried in the wood. On which account he was flogged out of the town.

192. October 9th. Anna Maria Schwerdt-mennin a thief from Weyssmann, mistress of the executed Jew whom she had helped in his thefts and murders. She was to be executed on Saturday, but protested against the sentence because she was with child, and was flogged out of the town. On the 10th of July of the year 1592 she had been so flogged, together with her lover. (*See Part II., No.* 180.)

194. December 11th. Anna Arnoldin, a peasant wench (servant) was brought here from Lauff, because she had secretly borne a child, which she had thrust under the bedclothes with the intention of suffocating it. But her mistress found it, so that it was baptized, although it died immediately after. Flogged out of the town.

Year 1595

209. September 25th. Ursula Grimin, other-wise called Ploben (Plauen?) landlady of the

Rotenherz in St. Lawrence Square, a prostitute, bawd, and procuress, because she had often committed adultery; had prostituted her serving maids; was skilled in enticing men to lechery; used to catch them by the cloak and say she was a wet nurse and knew which man could beget a child. On which account she was stood in the pillory; flogged as far as the stocks, there branded on both cheeks, and afterwards whipped thence out of the town.

Year 1596

214. July 3rd. Hans Hübner, a countryman, brought in here from Ayldorf, being reputed to be one who had attacked people for the purpose of having unnatural sexual intercourse with them. Flogged out of the town.

217. November 10th. Endress (Andrew) Petry, otherwise known as Schweitzer, a citizen and goldsmith, because, in collusion with others he had taken wax impressions of iron keys for the purpose of robbery; had sworn violently; defamed an honourable Council with insulting expressions; had caused two false conveyances

of house property to be drawn up ; and by an interchange of Bastian Unterholtzer's and Göss-wein's seals had contrived to get duplicates of them made, though no one was swindled by this device. Moreover, he had stolen 2,000 florins from Herr Mayl, town official of Worms; spoken ill of the same man's mother and wife, and compelled the women to acknowledge their guilt. Flogged out of the town.

Year 1597

220. October 5th. Nicholas Herzog of Schauenstein, a clerk, who at Hoff in Voitland had got a maid with child, promising to marry her, but left her in the lurch when she was pregnant. He also got a maid with child at Wehr, and married her. Flogged out of the town.

Year 1598

224. May 8th. Veit Willet of Gunterspiel, who had cheated many people through dealing with them in horses, was banished for life from the town and the district within ten miles of

the same. Which he was compelled to swear to do. (*See Part I., No.* 194.)

Year 1599

227. February 16th. Hans Rössner of Nuremberg, who had eight times broken the Ban, and on February 5th, 1586, had been lashed out of the town, once more returned to it, and worshipped an image. The street boys objected to this, saying that Herr Schollhamer in his sermons declared this was wrong, and that one should learn to pray to God instead. Thereupon he called Herr Schöllhamer a Calvinistic rogue and a thief ; said that what the man preached was a lie; and that if a mere schoolboy should stand in the pulpit he would prove better instructed than that preacher. On which account, and because he had broken the Ban, two of his fingers were cut off.

228. March 9th. Stephen Reutter, of Nuremberg, a carpenter, otherwise known as Plob (Plauer), a member of the fighting order of St. Mark, and a free man at arms, having frequented the Prendtherr's place, got his daughter into trouble, promising her marriage. Finally when

she had been in this condition for ten or twelve weeks, he advised her to make use of something, and to take it to get rid of her trouble. For this purpose she suggested *juniperus sabina*, and gave him two batzen. He contrived to procure her some, and helped her mother to brew it ; often exhorted her to take it, and asked her whether she had used it. Finally as it would not work, he told her it was useless, she was to take no more, and that if she did any harm to the child he would reveal the matter ; and also that in Wilbad he had four times lain with the mother in her bed, wearing only his shirt, the daughter and nurse being privy to the fact. For which reason, as a favour, he was merely flogged out of the town.

230. August 17th. Hans Rau von Rossn, Anna his wife, Margaret his mother, Barbara his sister, four gypsies by blood ; because the wife had told fortunes to, and nursed a peasant woman of Obernbührlein who had been ill. The gipsy had robbed this woman of some 60 florins ; had robbed others, and also cheated them by telling fortunes. All four, by favour, merely whipped out of the town. The sister

was to have been married, and the wedding was to have taken place at Eger.

Year 1600

232. January 10th. Hans Spinler, otherwise known as the Devil's lad, a citizen of this town, and formerly landlord of the Scheer on the Fühl ; and Caspar Böham, a butcher. Spinler, because he had contrived false casks to which he fixed funnels full of brandy, the casks being filled with water, so that people were swindled. He had, moreover, in company with Böhem and others, such as Veit Willet, deceived folk when purchasing horses from them. In 1598, Böham had been flogged out of Vorchaim, on the grounds of his association with Chris Neuner, who was executed at Eschenau, when they stole a horse by riding away on it, as previously mentioned. (*See Part I., Nos.* 183, 194.)

1603

248. June 7th. Hannss Spiss, who was my intimate friend (? godfather) ; because he, when Jacob Pfister, a barber, murdered his wife, did not hinder the murderer, but ran away. Flogged out of the town by the *Löwe*.

Year 1609

261. February 23rd. Margaret Schreimeri of Megeldorff an old beggar woman of some sixty years, who had at various times deceived people, alleging the Pretfelde (lady) had given her a certain sum of money, namely two thousand florins, which she would give to whoever treated her kindly. She feigned illness, received the sacrament, and borrowed fifty florins from Herr Mayrn, parson and lord of Megeldorf; from Mayrn she also borrowed a cloak worth twenty-six florins, and a bracelet from his wife. (When asked for these valuables) she said she kept her money in the Schmiedt Gasse (Smith's Street), they must convey her thither, as she wished to give them the money during her life-time. So the clergyman walked by the carriage and comforted her; but when they came to the place, she fell down in a fit and said no word; causing people to stand round her discomfited. So too, in the places where she pretended to be ill, she got people to bring food and drink out to her, and received from them about twenty florins on the promise the money should be returned to them. On which

account she was branded on both cheeks as a swindler.

Year 1611

273. September 7th. Margaret Kleinin of Winsshaim, a house thief, also Merrta (Martha) Klauti, having broken open a cupboard and stolen twenty-six florins out of it, many tin (pewter) and copper utensils, begged of people, rattled bits of glass in a bag as if there were money inside, thinking to gain people's confidence thereby so that they might rob them; and having also committed many thefts at Einsshaim, were forbidden the city, and flogged out of it.

Year 1612

275. June 7th. Si(e)mon Schiller, *alias* Poten Si(e)mon, and Juliana his wife, because he had been a brothel keeper, and had himself practised lechery; was likewise an informer. His wife was a bawd; both had prostituted their daughter for money, and their niece had carried on much unchaste traffic. On this account both were whipped out of the town, but when they

had passed the city gate the citizens stoned the man to death. It was almost a year to a day that he had previously been stoned by the people, so that to save his life he had leapt into the water and crept into the machinery of the mill; otherwise he would then have been pelted to death. Each one of these two had brought the other to the *Loch* so that they might be imprisoned.

279. Lienhardt Dischinge of Greta, from Bavaria; who by forged letters and seals pretended to be an exiled Schoolmaster or Priest in the diocese of Bamberg, at Maurbach. Flogged out of the town.

INDEX I

ESSAY AND INTRODUCTION

INDEX II

A BRIEF LIST OF NAMES IN THE DIARY